KICKING OUT. HE...

A junior coach's diary of the 1999-2...

by Mark Currie

Photographs by John Hutchinson
Foreword by Geoffrey Richmond

The Parrs Wood Press
MANCHESTER

First Published in 2000

This book is copyright under the Berne Convention. All rights are reserved. Apart from any fair dealing for the purpose of private study, research, criticism or review, as permitted under the Copyright Act 1956, no part of this publication may be reproduced, stored in a retrieval system, or transmitted in any form or by any means electronic, electrical, chemical, mechanical, optical, photocopying, recording or otherwise without the prior permission of the copyright owner. Enquiries should be sent to the publishers at the undermentioned address.

THE PARRS WOOD PRESS
St Wilfrid's Enterprise Centre,
Royce Road, Manchester M15 5BJ
www.parrswoodpress.com

©Mark Currie 2000

ISBN 1903158 125

Printed by:

Fretwell Print and Design
Healey Works
Goulbourne Street
Keighley
West Yorkshire BD21 1PZ

For my brothers, Paul and Dave

The Author

Mark Currie was born in Burnley on 28th January 1960. He grew up in Lancashire before living and working as an advertising art director in London. He has since lived in Cairo and Bristol, before moving north to Otley in 1994, with his partner Julie and their three children, Joe, Maisie and Jimmy. He started the Otley Town Under 7s in 1997 and gained his F.A. Coaching Certificate the following year. He now works as a freelance art director/designer.

Acknowledgements

This book has taken over a large part of my life over the past few months. I have enjoyed the experience, although I would not have achieved my goal but for the support and contribution of a number of individuals.

To my dad for taking me to my first match and giving me the football bug. To my brothers, for all those wonderful days on the parks and football fields, even when no one else was there. To my mum for always washing my kit and giving me my self-belief that anything is possible if you try hard enough. To Joe and Jimmy for giving me reason to start the coaching. And to Julie and Maisie for just putting up with it all.

Obviously, without the boys in the Under 9s squad, there would have been no book at all, so I thank each and every one of them for making it such a memorable year. The same goes to their parents for being so supportive.

To Andy Searle, of The Parrs Wood Press, for his enthusiasm and encouragement and for saving me the agony of self-publishing. Thanks also to Pete Barran for proof reading the text and Steve Lunn for helping me sort out the design, artwork, typography and goodness knows what else.

My biggest thanks though goes to John Hutchinson. I cannot put a value on the number of hours he has unselfishly given over to help me, or the huge contribution his fantastic colour photographs make to the book. I am eternally grateful.

Foreword

There are millions who believe that the great game of football begins and ends in the Premiership. What everybody should understand is that without Otley Town Juniors and the thousands of other junior sides, there would be no professional football in the country.

The real heros of football are not Sir Alex Ferguson, Arsene Wenger, etc., but Mark Currie, part-time coach for Otley Town Juniors and his counterparts up and down the land.

Being a professional footballer is perhaps the dream of all young boys, but the reality is that only a very small percentage actually realise their dream. The true benefit of junior sport is that it provides an interest which is very positive and in many ways is the perfect antidote to a lot of the problems that exist in society.

I commend the book that Mark Currie has written as a valuable work which should be read and enjoyed from cover to cover.

GEOFFREY RICHMOND, Chairman, Bradford City

In the summer of 1970, when Everton were the First Division Champions and England were defending the World Cup in Mexico, I became a football manager for the first time. I was ten years old.

My team was Everpool, an entirely fictitious outfit of invented players, made to play a game that was a cross between Table Soccer and Subbuteo. The players were all highly talented internationals: Steve Templeman, Tony Harvey, Joe Capello and the non-stop-man-of-motion, Jimmy Ball (no relation to my boyhood idol Alan Ball, but from the same mould).

I made the game from the flip side of the green felt Subbuteo 'grass' stretched over a piece of cardboard and on top of a slab of hardwood. All the touchlines, the centre circle and goal areas were marked out with a white chinagraph pencil. This faded over time and needed re-marking by the groundsman. The goalposts were white straws stuck together with sellotape and draped over with a fine green netting mesh. The players were Ludo figures and the ball a tiddlywink, though sometimes a button.

I played my team of all-stars against all the First Division sides of the time and drew up league tables. There was the F.A. Cup to look forward to and even the odd international. All the matches were timed and accompanied by my own David Coleman-type commentary. I was in my element. And Everpool won the 'Double' in their first season.

******

Twenty-seven years later and well into the Indian summer of my own amateur playing career, I decided to retrace my steps and go into coaching for real. My eldest son Joe was already playing football, so it was natural for me to want to encourage his younger brother Jimmy to play as well. I took an F.A. Coaching course and started the Under 7s age group at Otley Town Football Club.

For the first year I only coached the boys on a Saturday morning, introducing a couple of friendly matches towards the end of the season. The following year, I entered two teams into the Norman Bairstow Friendly League, with qualified success. My A team finished eighth in a league of ten, whilst the B team finished bottom of their division, losing every match. However, we'd played well in enough matches to lead me to believe that next season could be different. This is the story of that season.

******

1

Jack Wood

Otley Town Juniors Under 9s
Date of Birth: *4th April 1991*
Position: *Midfield*
Nickname: *Five*
Favourite football team: *Man. Utd*
Favourite food: *Fish & chips*
Favourite drink: *Orange juice*
Best thing outside football:
My Playstation
What I'll be when I'm grown up:
A footballer

* * * * *

Max Milner

Otley Town Juniors Under 9s
Date of Birth: *25th September 1990*
Position: *Defender*
Nickname: *Pepsi*
Favourite football team: *Leeds Utd*
Favourite food: *Pizza*
Favourite drink: *Lemonade*
Best thing outside football:
My Playstation
What I'll be when I'm grown up:
A footballer

* * * * *

Saturday 10th July.
Pre-season planning.

In September 1999, the English F.A. officially launch its implementation of Mini-Soccer for all children at all levels. The game introduces a maximum number of seven players competing on smaller pitches up to 60 x 40 yards with scaled down goalposts (12' x 6'). This mandate is something I totally support, having experienced first hand the benefits of small-sided football for my own boys during last season. Mini-Soccer meets the needs of the young, unlike the 11 v 11 game that I was brought up on during my school days.

Back in the 1970s, playing into full-sized goals on a huge pitch was often an exhausting and unfulfilling experience. Certainly, if you weren't one of the better players, or if you played on the wing, you were lucky to even touch the ball more than a few times. With only seven boys on each side playing on a smaller pitch, every player gets plenty of opportunity to get lots of touches on the ball and be involved, without it being too physically demanding.

The most important thing for children learning to play football is for them to enjoy the game. All too often in this country they are brought up fearing the backlash of failure. Skills must be encouraged. Kicking the ball anywhere requires no skill at all and so educating the parents is part of the process. Anyone ranting and raving, urging boys to get rid of it, does nothing but harm. Individual talent has to be nurtured and allowed to develop, without fear of making mistakes. Fortunately, the parents of my boys seem to respect this. The 'get stuck in' attitude prevalent in the British game is surely a prehistoric philosophy which only perpetrates deficiencies in our football.

One of the things I've learnt since completing my F.A. Coaching Certificate, is the importance of cultivating the right attitude in my young players. Winning is not and should not be the criteria by which success is judged. This isn't always easy, but by creating an environment that encourages a player to develop his own techniques and self-awareness without having to win, will almost certainly enhance that player's potential in the long term. It makes sense also that self-motivated players will make more effective players, thinking for themselves and taking responsibility for their actions. This is a gradual process. At a very young age, players need to be told what to do a lot of the time. However, coaching by asking questions can be a powerful tool in the way the individual and team develop.

The new junior league season is still two months away, but I've arranged the first coaching session for next week. This will hopefully enable one or two new players to get involved for a few weeks before I start in earnest in August.

My aims this season are simple.
1. Continue to help develop each and every one of the boys in the Under 8 and the Under 9 age groups, both individually and as a team. 2. Have a training plan for the season - something I can measure the boys' progress against. This plan will be kick-started with a 'Summer Coaching Week' designed to cover a broad range of skills, from basic ball control and passing, to shooting, heading and goalkeeping. 3. Develop my own abilities and experience as a coach by attending sessions put on by those more experienced than myself, as well as getting some of those people to give their time to coaching my lads at Otley Town. 4. Make it all as much fun as possible. For me, much as I'd love to help cultivate an all conquering team of boy wonders, if the majority are still playing when they've left school at sixteen or eighteen, I'd feel as if I'd achieved something. It would show me that as well as being quite good at it, they're almost certainly continuing to enjoy what I consider the world's greatest game.

Saturday 17th July.

My first coaching session prior to the new season and within twenty minutes I've reduced a boy to tears.

It's a lovely sunny day and feeling all rested and raring to go after a six week break from football, I greet the sixteen boys who have turned up. There are five new faces. Two of the younger ones, Charlie Hopkinson and James Caton, I already know through friends and both look to be quite useful players. Of the other boys, two are complete beginners by the look of things and the fifth lad, Adam, is a giant, next to any of my current Under 9s. He could become my white football-playing Jona Lumu, if he's any good. There appears to be a good atmosphere and I am certainly enjoying being back coaching again. After a suitably upbeat warm-up I notice one of the new younger boys, Matthew, looking a little lost, so I go up to him and offer a few words of encouragement. Unfortunately, he just bursts into tears for no apparent reason. As his mother has left him with me, I start to wonder how to placate him, until Alex Hawley, who somehow knows him, comes to the rescue. Whatever he says seems to do the trick and within minutes, Matthew is enjoying himself again, tears forgotten.

Alex is a great little character. Just to look at him makes me laugh sometimes. During a match at Bolton Woods last season, he failed to arrive for the kick-off and was therefore made substitute. However, he was obviously eager to play, as a few minutes later I could see him from a distance arriving with his mother. As he ran over to the pitch I noticed something different about him and was temporarily distracted from the match that had already begun. His hair was gelled-up into the most

amazing quiff at the front. I couldn't believe what I was seeing, so his mother Clare explained, slightly embarrassed, that it was a style like "Joey from Friends", the American hit comedy.

Another time, at training, as I was attempting to explain a certain passing technique, Alex, for reasons known only to himself, began girating his hips madly to the side of me, putting me off and reducing everyone else to hysterical laughter.

Sunday 18th July.

One or two administration tasks. I phone round some of the other Otley Junior managers, on the scrounge for some spare strips for next season. Last year, I had enough kit for two teams, but this season I need extra for the Under 8s. I also need a couple of sets of the Samba goalposts for my Summer Coaching Week in August. Not much joy with the kit as yet.

Thursday 22nd July.

Peter Smith phones up and we get into a long conversation about his son, Martin. Peter is a nice guy, but he can talk for England. There's no such thing as a quick chat. Pull up a chair and settle in for the evening.

I could write a whole book about Martin Smith alone. He's a lovely lad and another real character, if not the most naturally gifted with a ball. Having said that, he's always at training with a smile on his face and appears to listen to what I'm saying. Put him in a match situation however and the unexpected happens.

He's quite a big lad for his age, so in our first ever game against local rivals, Weston Lane, I made him goalkeeper. All was well for a couple of minutes - until he touched the ball. Then a shot went through his legs. Another went through his hands, but

wide of the post. He made a save. Then another. One shot hit him on the shins and rebounded off to safety. At half-time, we were 7-0 down. Then mid-way through the second half he must have got very bored. Either that or the person he was talking to was deliberately distracting him, because as the ball sped towards goal and into the net, Martin was looking the other way, leaning on a post.

In my post-match notes, I remarked, "Martin must learn to concentrate and use the basic skills of goalkeeping, i.e. hands."

In our second match at home to Whinmore, I played him in defence. Ten minutes into the game and following a strong challenge on an unsuspecting opponent, I tried telling him to be more careful in the tackle. As I spoke and he nodded in agreement, Martin walked backwards into Stuart Smith, one of my smallest boys, who was tying his shoe lace, so trampling on his head and making him cry.

And when it was time to vote for the Players' Player of the Year at the end of last season, Martin wanted to vote for himself, until his dad explained that that wasn't the point. "But it's me, Dad!" shouts Martin, "I am the Player of the Year!"

Saturday 24th July.

Today is very blustery. The breeze makes it difficult to be heard. Thank god for whistles! Keeping control is crucial when dealing with young boys. And there are several tinkers among this group, that if given an inch cause mayhem. Ironically, the smallest lad of all is probably the most mischievous: Andrew Kendall. Whenever there is trouble, Andrew is there. Wherever there is mud, Andrew slides in it. Whenever there's an opportunity to go missing, Andrew's out of sight. His little gang of 'dirty angels' often includes my own son, Jimmy and Sean Brotherton.

Last season, on a particularly rainy Thursday evening, the "Three Amigos" decided the shooting drill wasn't exciting enough and went 'off skidding.' Within minutes of sliding about in the thick muddy goalmouth they were covered in the stuff. I laughed at the looks on their mothers' faces when they came to take their sons home - until I realised one little mud man was coming home with me!

At the end of today's session, I give out letters to all the parents and collect in monies for the Summer Coaching Week. I'm already praying for dry weather.

Saturday 31st July.

A very, very hot one. And on days like these, plans go out the window. It's a day to be flexible, with plenty of drink stops. Some heading practice, some small sided games and some- let's-all-enjoy-the-summer. With a blink of an eye it'll soon be wet, cold and November. Today's session is mentally re-scheduled for another day.

Adam Walker

Otley Town Juniors Under 9s
Date of Birth: 7th November 1990
Position: *Defender*
Nickname: *Daddy Long Legs*
Favourite football team: *Man. Utd*
Favourite food: *Fish & chips*
Favourite drink: *Orange Tango*
Best thing outside football:
My Playstation
What I'll be when I'm grown up:
A footballer

* * * * *

Louis Christoforou

Otley Town Juniors Under 9s
Date of Birth: 31st October 1990
Position: *Midfield*
Nickname: *Toffee*
Favourite football team: *Bradford*
Favourite food: *Pasta*
Favourite drink: *Dr Pepper*
Best thing outside football:
Rollerblading
What I'll be when I'm grown up:
A footballer

* * * * *

AUGUST

Sunday 1st August.
Summer Coaching Week.

After much organising - setting out a plan for the week, arranging help, including a fully-qualified professional coach for three of the mornings, the cutting of the grass at Otley Town Football Club and confirming the use of the clubhouse, borrowing two sets of Samba goals, the designing and printing of T-shirts marking the event, buying enough prizes to give out during the week, arranging a tour round Leeds United and a bus to take us there - I am ready for a holiday! I only hope the weather holds.

Monday 2nd August.

Despite having had little or no sleep the night before, I'm up early and have the car loaded up by 8.00am. It includes: forty markers, twenty-six footballs, twenty-odd bibs, two pumps, eight traffic cones, one set of Samba goals with nets, a box full of prizes for the week, packed lunches for myself and my two sons Joe and Jimmy, enough water and juice to fill several large bottles (two frozen) and the day's session plan.

I'm at and inside the clubhouse for 9.15am, instantly cursing the person responsible for setting the alarm without telling me the code to turn the damn noise off. After twenty minutes of phoning round, the magic number is discovered and the terrible 'wailing' subsides. Full-time coach, Phil Ovington arrives. He is taking the morning's session, with today's emphasis on passing and running with the ball. Steve Milner is also here, thank goodness. He is helping me all day every day this week. I wonder if he really knows what he's let himself in for. Come to that, do I?

By 10.00am, it is already very hot outside and all the boys have turned up with bags, boots, packed lunches and drinks. There are twenty-six lads in total: ten Under 8s, ten Under 9s and six older (two Under 10s and four Under 11s).

After taking the register and laying down one or two rules for the week, it's out on to the pitch, where I introduce the boys to Phil and he takes control.

By lunchtime, after a reasonably successful morning, all the boys are hot, thirsty and hungry. So we break for half an hour and I bandy a few nicknames about. Jack Wood has four older brothers, all of whom play football for Otley Town. When he was born, Joanne and Simon, his mum and dad apparently ran out of ideas for names, so for a while he went by the name of "Five." Among the others, Max Milner becomes "Pepsi" and Lloyd Almond is "Ja Ja Nuts."

After lunch it's harder to keep the boys focused and by the end of the afternoon, everyone wants a cool sponge down and a sit in the shade. Andrew Kendall goes one step further and tips a bucket of water over Arran Danskin's head.

Tuesday 3rd August.

One of the most difficult tasks for a junior football coach is to organise and conduct a practice session. Not only do numbers vary from eight to twenty-odd, you can guarantee there will never be the same number at two sessions running. This week is slightly different. I know the numbers, but it is especially important to sustain interest and enthusiasm over the whole day, whilst still practising meaningful situations.

I can't afford to pay Phil for more than three mornings, so today I only have Steve helping me. We work on ball control and incorporate turning with the ball. It is another hot day and some of the younger lads are struggling in the heat. So we break early for lunch and try keeping them all inside the clubhouse for as long as possible. Rejuvenated, we practise turning and shooting with backs to goal in the afternoon. This is followed by a 'golden goal' shoot-out: five seconds to run thirty yards with the ball, before trying to score into the net. The game is 'sudden death': if you miss, you're out. Unfortunately, someone has upset Alex Hawley and he's decided to pack his bags and set off for home. I shout for him to come back, which he does, but only after some careful negiotiations from his big brother Jamie. And so with emotions running high, Alex Hawley goes on to win the shoot-out amidst jubliant scenes. From tears to cheers, he stands, in his red Manchester United shirt, arms aloft, mobbed by boys he's just fallen out with. You'd think he'd scored the winning goal in the World Cup Final.

Wednesday 4th August.

I wake up before the alarm clock, anticipating a good day. They say goalkeepers are mad and goalkeepers are different. Jimmy is our family's dose of the unexpected. The sort of child that rebels against the norm, questions authority and generally seems to have a 'left field' approach to life. His idea of fun is to wear his underpants on top of his head, so he ought to be a natural in goal. Phil Ovington is back to co-ordinate the practice and I also have Adie Atter, the Otley Town senior goalkeeper there to help. We set up four of the Samba goals in a line across the pitch. After a period of going through the basic handling and positioning techniques, the boys split off into their own age groups and deal with shot stopping and narrowing the angle. The emphasis has to be on the boy between the posts, but the session allows the rest to take plenty of shots on goal. Everyone gets a chance to practise their goalkeeping skills and it certainly occupies all until well after 12 o'clock. Phil and Adie then go, leaving Steve and I in charge of the crazy gang over lunch. Two of the boys' parents, Bev Beecroft and Ian Simm stick around to help keep the peace.

With the weather still nice and warm, the afternoon is more about fun: a game of 'crab football.' This is a crazy game, played shuffling around on your backside, using arms as back legs, whilst trying to kick the ball in the general direction of the goal. It comes as light relief from the more structured coaching stuff and creates lots of laughs. We finish off with a penalty competition and some small-sided games. From my point of view, the best day so far.

Thursday 5th August.

Shock! Horror! It's drizzling rain this morning. I'd kind of got used to days being hot and dry. Despite the grim weather, Phil conducts his last practice, a suitably lively and varied session, demonstrating the basic

11

heading techniques. Diving headers are very popular, not surprisingly. Even boys previously nervous about heading, embrace the practice and enjoy it. Some of them even open their eyes whilst doing it! Come twelve o'clock, I thank Phil for his excellent contribution during the week and the boys give him a round of applause. For them, I think it has been good to practise with another coach other than myself. It's also given me plenty of ideas of my own, as well as reminding me how much I still have to learn as a football coach.

In the afternoon, we have the aerial equivalent of a penalty shoot-out - a heading competition. Then it's time to pack up early, ready for the trip to Leeds United. This is something most of the boys have been looking forward to since early this morning. On the coach, there's a lot of singing and shouting from the boys, who are all excited, particularly the Leeds supporters among them. We arrive shortly before 3pm and after a word with John Holmes, the Promotions Manager, a friend of mine who's laid on the tour, we're all shown round the football ground, including a trip inside the dressing rooms and a view pitch-side, sat in the dug-outs. Amazingly, no one runs on to the pitch itself, not even Andrew Kendall.

Friday 6th August.

The last day and sunshine has returned. Steve and I set up the Samba goals for the morning's session, which is on shooting. All the lads enjoy the opportunity to score a goal or two and just before twelve o'clock, I coach the technique of the

overhead kick. This is especially well received, even distracting a few from their favourite pastime, 'lunch'.

In the afternoon, I engage the boys in several 'crazy' relays, by way of fun. This is followed by a goalkeeping competition for the three age groups, the winner being the one to save the most spot kicks. With the odd bit of controversy and a few disappointed tears on the faces of one or two losers, the eventual winners are Oliver (Under 8s), Jack (Under 9s) and Barney (Under 10s & 12s). A mad all-in match completes the week, with Steve and I taking the goalkeeping roles. The excitement eventually gets the better of me and I get the winning goal for the 'blue bibs', crashing home a penalty past the motionless Mr Milner.

The last prizes are given out, along with mini footballs and I thank all the boys for coming and generally behaving themselves during the week. One or two bottles of wine, etc. come my and Steve's way, which we're almost as grateful for as the course being finally over!

Saturday 14th August.

After a week's rest, I return to action. It's a low turnout, with quite a few boys away on holiday. My own family are in Scotland, which means no Jimmy today. I haven't gone because of work commitments. Instead, in warm sunshine, a good little session on dribbling - something I wasn't able to cover in the Summer Coaching Week.

Tuesday 17th August.

Tonight, I agree a fixture with Burley Juniors' manager David Crane at Otley Football Club on Sunday 29th August. These will be the first friendly matches prior to the season, for both age groups. Hopefully, I'll be able to organise at least one more before the league programme begins.

Saturday 21st August.

Quite a warm day and a better attendance than last week. Defending is the topic of the day, something I haven't worked on specifically before. Most of the boys try their best, though it's always frustrating when the odd one messes about and distracts the others. On a particular Thursday evening last season, at

Chippendale school gym, some of the lads were getting carried away and balls started flying around. Before I could get order, there was a tremendous crash and the gymnasium clock fell spectacularly from the wall, scattering glass pieces everywhere. Matthew Waring, the guilty party, looked rather sheepish, but I found it hard to blame him specifically, when it could have happened to any one of them. This kind of situation usually ends up, like today, with me getting all the boys together 'for a chat.' Sometimes, I have to remind them for the need to behave. I certainly get no pleasure from shouting at them, as it gets in the way of the main purpose, which is playing football.

Today also marks the first win of the season for my beloved Everton - 4-1 at home to Southampton, which puts me in a good mood for the evening.

Wednesday 25th August.
Annual League Meeting.

Eddie Presland is a rather unique character. He has no children of his own, yet spends inordinate amounts of time organising and running the Norman Bairstow Junior Football League. All the administration is done by him alone, including the fixtures for one hundred and fifty teams over five age groups and this year, sorting out individual identity cards for each and every one of the boys playing in the league. All the results for all of the matches are taken by a dedicated answerphone service, between twelve o'clock and 4pm on a Sunday and calls are often taken personally when the need arises.

This year's meeting is at the rugby ground of the Keighley Cougars. Typically, as I've never been there before, I get lost driving around the town and arrive late. There is a large attendance listening to Eddie relaying information on this season's league structure and all managers are given a programme detailing the rules, contact numbers and fixtures for the year. I drink a pint of Guinness and deliberate on our first game against Nabb Wood on Sunday 12th September.

Saturday 28th August.

Today, I work on showing the boys how to create space for themselves, before and after receiving a pass. The Under 9s quickly grasp the practice and are soon zipping the ball around the grid with confidence. It works slightly less well with the younger boys - their ball control and passing sometimes letting them down.

Afterwards, a quick dash home for lunch, before resuming the umpteenth season in my own diminishing playing career. (Hope my injured knee, ankle, blistered toes, etc. etc. don't let me down.)

Sunday 29th August.
Home to Burley Juniors.

It's a sunny day and I'm up and about getting things ready for our first matches of the season, still aglow from my own spectacular twenty-five yard chipped goal in yesterday's 5-2 victory for Otley Town reserves. At 9.45am, I'm at the club having a major disagreement with the often temperamental dry line marker. Today it is totally useless and at first does not make a white line at all. When I

13

try to fiddle with it, the lid falls off, spilling a massive heap of white powder all over the place. This gives me a hot head and even less time to complete the job of putting up the nets. Fortunately, one or two parents come to the rescue and by 11.00 am we're kicking off the Under 9s fixture on time.

The team starts very slowly, despite an outstanding first half by Jack Wood and the missing of at least two clear cut chances. At half-time, Burley lead 1-0. I sit the boys down at the break, let them have a drink and point out how they might improve. In the second half we play much better and goals from Sean, Michael and Murray give us a 3-1 win, though there are several opportunities to add to the score. A good debut from Matthew McGlinchey, one of the new boys, helps to give the promising start I'd hoped for.

Even better was to come, with the Under 8s. Minus the influential Joe Driver, Alex Hawley and Oliver Comyn, all absent, they win 6-1. Sam 'Big Man' Richmond gets a hat-trick, whilst Arran Danskin, James Caton and James Dalby - another new player - score the other goals.

The two funniest moments of the day however, belong to the one and only Martin Smith. After a quiet first half in goal, I change the team round in the second half, allowing Martin to play in defence. For ten minutes he does nothing wrong. All of a sudden, with the ball in front of him, but facing his own goal, Martin tries a pile-driver which is destined for the bottom corner of his own net. At the same time, the previously injured Charlie re-enters the fray from behind the goal, neatly controls the aforementioned shot and clears it out of harm's way. Minutes later, the Under 8s are on the defensive again. A bullet of a shot from a Burley forward strikes a post, flies across goal and is met by the head of the unfortunate Martin, speeding it into the unguarded net. I smile at him from my position behind the goal, whilst he rubs his head and looks at me wondering what the heck has happened!

Tuesday 31st August.

Last season, I ran two sides at Under 8. A meeting with all the boys' parents at the end of May, determined that the youngest of the boys could play another year in the same age group. Paul Danskin offered to look after that team on match days, leaving me to run two teams at Under 9. Today, due to personal commitments, Paul tells me he cannot take on the job. This leaves me with a problem. The Under 9s are playing in the Norman Bairstow League, as last year, but the Under 8s are entered into the newly formed Wharfedale League. Obviously, I can't be in two places at once on Sundays, nor would I have the time or energy. The options are simple: 1. Find a new manager or persuade one or two of the parents to take on the responsibility. 2. Not have an Under 8s team. (This would break my heart after all the time and effort I've put in the last two seasons, so it simply can't be an option.)

Later, I phone Mark Hardcastle of Weston Lane Juniors, to arrange a friendly for this Saturday morning. He thinks it'll be OK, but says he'll ring to confirm tomorrow.

Matthew McGlinchey

Otley Town Juniors Under 9s
Date of Birth: 15th October 1990
Position: Forward
Nickname: Dude
Favourite football team: Man. Utd
Favourite food: Beef
Favourite drink: Dr Pepper
Best thing outside football:
Playing cricket
What I'll be when I'm grown up:
A footballer

* * * * *

Murray Simm

Otley Town Juniors Under 9s
Date of Birth: 1st April 1991
Position: Midfield or forward
Nickname: Mints
Favourite football team: Leeds Utd
Favourite food: Beef
Favourite drink: Cola
Best thing outside football:
Playing cricket
What I'll be when I'm grown up:
A footballer

* * * * *

Wednesday 1st September.

Mark Hardcastle confirms the matches for the Under 9s on Saturday morning. Not sure whether there will be a game for our Under 8s, as he hasn't been able to make contact with the Weston Lane Under 8s manager. Spend a good half an hour to an hour phoning round my parents re-directing them from the usual training session venue at Otley Town, to Weston Lane for 10.00am.

Thursday 2nd September.

Following a telephone conversation with Peter Smith, Martin's dad, he has agreed to be manager for the Under 8s. This is good news, as well as a weight off my mind. However, I will still be coaching the two age groups on training days for the time being.

Saturday 4th September.
Away to Weston Lane.

A hot day, even at 9.00am. I meet all my lads and their parents at Weston Lane, which is a hive of activity. Their Under 8s and Under 10s are at training, with their Under 9s due to play against us. All in all I have thirteen boys, plus a lad called Andrew Newlove, who I've never seen play or train before. His dad phoned the other night, so I'll try him out in the second match. Of the rest, Matthew Waring hasn't turned up, Adam is suffering from a sore knee and David is on holiday.

Weston Lane have a good side and enjoy a little more possession than we do, though the game is fairly close. It's therefore disappointing for us that the home side score twice before half-time. Both are quite soft goals with one going in off keeper Chris Baker's face. At the break I put Jimmy in goal and play Andrew Kendall in defence in his place. In the second half, we start to pass the ball a bit better as a team and pull a goal back through Michael Beecroft. Jimmy then pulls off a great diving save, before a miscued cross from a striker called Josh Waite, sails over

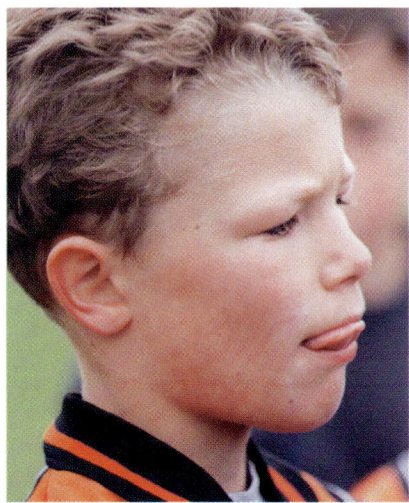

his head, leaving him helpless to stop a 3-1 final scoreline.

I'm more pleased with the performance than the result, especially the way we played in the second period. Last season we rarely competed with the good sides for more than half a game.

In the second match, we are for the most part under the cosh and rarely get forward. However, towards the end, a great run by new boy, James Dalby results in a penalty, after he is upended in the box. Murray "Mints" Simm crashes home from the spot, but it merely serves as consolation in a 4-1 defeat, which is about right on the day. The unknown quantity, Andrew Newlove, plays for a few minutes in the second half, before I take him off again. He looks a bit lost, which is not surprising. My mistake. I should have known better than to try someone before seeing him in training first. I also think the B team generally are going to require a lot of work before they start playing as a team. But it's early days and at least most of them have played a match before the first fixtures in the Norman Bairstow League next weekend.

Monday 6th September.

Rush from work to watch my eldest son, Joe, play for Otley Town Juniors Under 12s. Afterwards, I drop him off at home before going straight to the Junior managers meeting at the Summercross pub in Otley. The meeting is already under way, with Peter Smith there to represent the Under 8s. A match for the younger boys against Whinmore on Sunday, gives myself and Peter the opportunity to talk to all parents about the change in personnel.

Sunday 12th September.
Home to Nabb Wood.

On a warm sunny morning, I'm up, showered, had breakfast and down the club by 8.20am. The line marker is kind to me this morning, which is just as well given there are two pitches to mark out. Peter Smith turns up in good time to help me with the putting up of nets and completes the marking out of the Under 8s pitch.

Matthew Waring is the first of my Under 9s to arrive and helps set things up. He's a good lad and a great little footballer. Blessed with a good touch on the ball, he can also tackle as ferociously as any at that age I've come across. He can run all day and shoots with the power of a little Bobby Charlton. He is certainly one of the players I like to pencil into my team first.

The rest turn up by 10 o'clock, so we do a little warm up, as normal and I give the team a quick pep talk. Then it's kick off time. As usual, lots of parents are watching and I'm quietly confident. Last season, we were beaten 5-0 and 3-2 by Nabb Wood, but our lads have improved a lot in that time. So it turns out, with most of the play in the visitors' half. Nevertheless, it takes a fortuitous goal to break the deadlock. Jack Wood appears to handle the ball, before side-footing past the goal-keeper. A few parents from the Nabb Wood contingent shout out in disbelief, but the goal stands. (Perhaps not surprisingly, given the referee is Jack's dad, Simon!) At half-time, I swap my goalkeepers round - Sean Brotherton for Jimmy - and encourage more in the way of shooting. The second half is much the same as the first, only better. One brilliant move, with Matthew Waring back-heeling the ball for Michael Beecroft to cross first time and Matthew McGlinchey to head against a post, was the magic moment of a superb second period. Two more goals from Jack, two from Michael and another from Matthew McGlinchey seal our biggest ever win, 6-0. It's early days, but I couldn't have wished for a better start.

Then to really put a smile on my face, the B team win 5-1. This is more than I could have hoped for, especially considering the lack of practice some of these lads have had. Adam Walker has never played a match before in his life. He does well, as does James Dalby, who helps himself to a hat-trick. The other goals are scored by Toby Hall and Sean, who gets five minutes as a substitute, after hardly touching the ball as goalkeeper in the A team match.

The Under 8s win their games too, against Whinmore, so it's a good morning all round. In a way, it's strange to be relinquishing responsibility for the younger boys. I've coached most of them for two seasons now and grown quite attached to them.

After watching the last twenty minutes of the Under 12s match in another part of Otley (Joe's team winning 13-1), I get home, put all the gear away and phone in the results to Eddie Presland.

Monday 13th September.
Training night. New venue, at Wharfemeadow Fields. And on the back of the most successful results, if not performances so far, probably the biggest nightmare of a training session, ever.

'Always have a plan,' is my motto. Well, tonight it got blown to bits. The theory was fine, or so I thought, but a total of twenty-three boys turning up (both Under 8s, Under 9s and a few new faces besides) presented a number I hadn't expected. More than that, they all seem to have the 'Devil in their Eyes'. Twice during the warm-up, I sit down waiting for them to stop talking, pushing and generally larking about. I feel the anger rising inside me and ask them to behave themselves.

" I'm here to help you to enjoy and play better football. So if you want to learn, then listen. If you want to muck about, then go join a crèche." The warm-up lasts too long as a result and consequently I end up compromising the rest of the session.

Even more messing about hampers progress during the shooting drill. As a coach, there are so many opportunities to correct bad technique, I lose count. But instead of persevering, I give up and just let them get on with it, making me feel totally deflated and demoralised. I probably should have done better, but I'd defy anybody, professional or otherwise to control and make a session work when boys are in this sort of mood.

And at the height of my frustration comes the moment I discover dog dirt on the grass, right in the middle of the goalmouth. Now this is something that makes me angry at the best of times. Why do people let their dogs crap all over an area where children are going to play? Why can't they bloody well take it home or put it out of harm's way? I bet they don't let their dog do it in their own house or garden. So as Lloyd Almond and David Smith run towards goal, moments away from making a hash of another attempt on goal, I see red, pick up the filthy muck and hurl it as far as I possibly can. It's the sort of night that makes me question, "Why the hell am I doing this?"

Wednesday 15th September.

A night of phoning round and organising for the match on Sunday against Idle Juniors. Their manager is a guy called Wayne Potter, who I've never met because Otley haven't played against Idle before. Wayne tells me he's speaking from his bed when I

call (which is kind of unnerving). I take a set of vague directions from him on how to get to their ground and afterwards phone round my boys' parents, setting a meet time at Otley Town F.C. for 9.40am on Sunday morning, for those involved in the A team. The boys playing in the B team game will go straight to the ground for 11.00am. Finally, I call Peter Smith about arranging some regular support for myself on training nights. It's hard coaching so many boys on my own and eventually, it would be great if the Under 8s could be looked after separately. Perhaps I was a little ambitious at the start of the season, thinking I could combine the coaching of the two age groups. At the moment I feel responsible for all of them and so will continue to do the best I can for the time being.

Sunday 19th September. Away to Idle Juniors.

Another morning of complete and utter joy. After last season's maulings, two successive wins for both teams. First the A team, who take the home side to bits, scoring at will in the second half. At half-time, it's only 2-0, but by the finish, double figures would not have flattered us. In the end we win 8-0. Matthew W and Michael getting a hat-trick each, with Jack and Sean scoring the other goals.

My own, particularly satisfying moment of the match came with the scoring of our second goal. The home side were attacking at the time, when the ball was won in midfield and played to Michael on the halfway line. With one defender in front of him and Sean up in support, Michael took the wide route forward, before rolling the perfect pass to Sean, who had run into a position in front of goal. The finish was a formality. So maybe Monday's training session on shooting in pairs wasn't such a waste of time after all.

Whilst the A team's performance is almost beyond criticism, the B team take a while to get going. When Murray eventually puts us in front, I hope we take control. But the opposite happens. Suddenly, our defence goes missing - twice. Two goals are scored and at half-time we're losing 2-1. I reorganise the defence, putting Adam there with Chris and pushing Toby and Andrew Kendall into midfield. Midway through the second half we equalise through Murray again. Then James puts us in front and it looks like the game is over. Idle then score again, but right at the death, Murray slots home from inside the box to snatch the winner. A really great game to watch and a shame one side had to lose.

When I get home, Joe's team, the Under 12s have won, as have the Under 8s, which is a great start for Peter Smith. Even more amazing is that Everton have also won again, to climb up to 7th in the Premiership table - young Francis Jeffers getting the winner. Can all my teams possibly keep this going?

Monday 20th September.

It's been a long time coming, but this morning brought the darkest of dark clouds over Otley and the wettest of heavy down pours. Other parts of the country are worse effected with flood alerts and higher than normal river levels. Tonight's training looks like being a wash out. I pile twenty balls, forty markers, the bibs, bag and session plan into my car anyway. By late afternoon, it's stopped raining. By 5.45pm, I'm on my way to Otley, a thirty minute drive from work on a busy teatime. The clouds still look ominous as I set out the markers for the session, which tonight is on passing. Nineteen boys arrive and by the time we're warming up the rain is falling. Nobody seems to mind much and it kicks off a pretty good evening. Hardly a moment of bad behaviour, though I do chastise Andrew Kendall and banish him to the 'sin bin' for five minutes. But unlike last week, when I felt down and useless, I really felt I made a difference tonight. Which is all I want to do. This week I was able to set up a successful practice and also go in and correct poor technique when necessary.

Sunday 26th September.
Home to Long Lee.

I wake up this morning slightly hungover. At 8.45am, the club is deserted and overnight rain has all but erased the line markings from the pitch, where I played yesterday afternoon. The garage, where the line marker and goal nets are kept is locked up. I don't have a key, but the window to the changing rooms has a pane of glass missing. This enables me to climb in and open the garage door from the inside. I top up the line marker with more lime and head out to the pitch. The coloured markers, normally an invaluable aid in training sessions, come in handy as line guides and I mark out an area about 60 x 40 paces.

The white lines are so straight, I have to remind myself that I had too much to drink last night. Alan Cooper, the Under 10s manager arrives and puts up the goals and netting. His lads are on before mine, so I leave him to it and head off home to get Jimmy. Within half an hour, I'm back at the ground, where boys and parents are arriving. Shane Waring and Steve Jefferies will referee the two matches, so I organise the warm-up with the boys from the A team and give them a team talk. Bev Beecroft and Julie Brotherton kindly agree to organise a raffle to help raise a few pounds for the team fund.

Last season, Long Lee absolutely slaughtered us, home and away. In

four matches we conceded twenty-nine goals and scored only one.

To start with, today is different. We pass the ball around well, create chances and generally compete in a cracking match. Almost against the run of play we lose a goal, when a shot hits the crossbar and the rebound is forced into the net. At half-time, we may be 1-0 down, but deep down I'm delighted with the way things are going. Max Milner in particular is having a tremendous influence on things, as is Matthew Waring. Second half isn't so good. Long Lee play at a tempo my lads can't match. They score four times in quick succession and the match is over. Although we never give up, we don't score and the final result is 5-0 to them.

Afterwards I tell my lads not to be too down. Although we couldn't match Long Lee over a whole game, it was certainly a huge improvement on last season's performance.

The B team play as poorly in the first half, as the A team played well. Application and concentration is none existent. We give the ball away too easily. No one makes a tackle on the opposition. And no one marks anyone when they have the ball. As a result, we are 4-0 down at half-time and facing a massacre. I find myself losing my cool a bit, something I don't like doing. And I know I should be patient, especially with some of the new lads. I make changes to the team at half-time and suddenly, it's a different game. Adam is solid in defence, Jimmy tackles and makes runs from midfield, whilst Sean creates chances up front. The team doesn't score and Long Lee nick one more, but I'm not too disappointed. At least they put more effort in.

After everyone has gone and the goal nets are put back in the garage, I head off to watch Joe play for the Under 12s. He is outstanding and wins a huge bar of chocolate for being Man of the Match. To complete a hectic, but entertaining day, I take my family to Manchester, for a first experience of a professional ice-hockey match.

Monday 27th September.

The start of indoor training at Prince Henry's school gym. I don't particularly like being in an echoey sports hall, because you can't do the same things inside as you can on grass. And when the balls are all flying around, it's difficult to hear yourself think, let alone make yourself heard. Control of the group is indeed tricky.

Tonight, I've also got one eye on the impending Merseyside derby - kick-off 8.00 pm. (The very idea of an Everton v Liverpool match makes my insides churn.)

The training session works out OK, mainly because I'm organised and firm with the boys with regard to their behaviour. And I don't try anything too adventurous. Just some basic passing and control, combining a turn with the ball. There are about twenty-four lads, which is a large number for a gym. It means when I split the boys off into teams for the last part of the session, they can't all play at once. There just isn't the room. Overall though, it's a good night.

When I get home, Julie has gone out for the evening, so I have to sort the kids out and get them to bed. As I don't have Sky TV, I have to resort to listening to the match at Anfield on the radio, which is absolute torture. Jimmy and Maisie are just getting their pyjamas on when Kevin Campbell scores after only four minutes. Any chance of settling them down for an early night's sleep goes out the window, as I jump around the kitchen in crazy dance of delight. Eventually, I get the twins to bed, but only after reading them a story and when I return to the radio, Everton are still leading. I cook up a pasta meal and then eat it, whilst frantically pacing the kitchen floor. This is not good on the digestion, but after what seems like an eternity, the final whistle blows and the Blues have won. Everton are now up to 6th in the Premiership, though I can't believe we can keep this up with the size of the squad we've got.

Toby Hall

Otley Town Juniors Under 9s
Date of Birth: *20th December 1990*
Position: *Defender*
Nickname: *Time Bomb*
Favourite football team: *Leeds Utd*
Favourite food: *Burgers*
Favourite drink: *Fanta*
Best thing outside football:
Playing rugby
What I'll be when I'm grown up:
A rally driver

* * * * *

Lloyd Almond

Otley Town Juniors Under 9s
Date of Birth: *26th September 1990*
Position: *Midfield*
Nickname: *Ja Ja Nuts*
Favourite football team: *Man. Utd*
Favourite food: *Steak & kidney pie*
Favourite drink: *Shandy*
Best thing outside football:
Playing my saxaphone
What I'll be when I'm grown up:
A footballer

* * * * *

Saturday 2nd October.

9.30pm. Bev Hall phones to let me know that Toby can't play in the morning. Her family are in Ireland and won't be back in time for the match. This is a shame, as I'd planned to play Toby as goalkeeper for the B team. I think he might be quite good.

Sunday 3rd October.
Home to Gomersal.

A fine sunny Autumn morning and I wake up feeling good, the smell of football in my nostrils. Yesterday had been a good day too. I'd played as usual for Otley Town. We'd won and I'd even scored a couple of goals - something of a rarity.

Today, my lads don't perform as well as in previous weeks, but the A team still win 2-0. For a change, I play Jack in goal in the first half and he makes two good saves. Matthew McGlinchey then scores. This is followed a few minutes later by a good bit of quick thinking. Matthew Waring takes a short corner to Murray, who shoots and before the Gomersal defence know what's going on, the ball is in the net. He's a smart kid, Murray. He has an alert mind and his technique is excellent.

The B team get lucky. They never really looking like scoring, but the visitors just can't hit the net. When they do hit the target, Jimmy comes to the rescue, making save after save. Even the ones he misses either hit the post, or he grabs at the second attempt. So we manage a 0-0 draw. Lots of plusses though, including the continuing good form of James Dalby in midfield and Adam Walker, the self-appointed 'Daddy Long Legs', in defence.

Monday 4th October.

As I've taken today off as a holiday, I am able to get to the gym at Prince Henry's for six o'clock, a bit earlier than usual. This way, the Under 8s get

half an hour's football before the Under 9s arrive. Then, when the younger boys leave at seven o'clock, the older lads have the hall to themselves. If only I could do this every week. The middle half-hour is coaching for all the boys, which this week is on the art of running with the ball. I make sure they all do this task, first with their good foot and then with their weaker one. The practice works well. Martin Smith even puts on the perfect demonstration using his left foot!

At the end of the session I give out the team sheets for Sunday, as usual. I promise to get those boys who have been training, but who so far haven't played, a match next week. Then I notice Michael Beecroft in tears, hiding behind his mum, Bev. It appears I have mistakenly assumed he would not be available this weekend and is therefore not on the teamsheet. Bev did tell me their family were going away on holiday. Only not until next week. My mistake. So I apologise to Michael, reinstate him into the team and he gives me a big smile. Which is great, because Michael's a nice lad as well as being a good player. He was top goalscorer last season and we would have missed him against Shipley this weekend. When he learns to be a bit stronger on the ball, he'll be an even better footballer than he already is.

Sunday 10th October.
Home to Shipley.

I met my good friend, Suj on a train from Liverpool to Manchester, one night back in the late '70s. Everton had sneaked a 1-0 win against Darlington in the League Cup and we were both killing time reading the match programme. Both at college in Manchester, we got talking and we've been blues brothers ever since. The 1980s, in particular, saw many a train trip to football venues - from

Tottenham and Brighton, to Dublin and Rotterdam. And despite down-right glum beginnings in the early part of the decade, Everton picked themselves up to reach glorious heights in the middle-late 80s. The F.A. Cup, the Championship (twice) and the European Cup Winners Cup, all went to Goodison in the space of a few seasons. They were good times.

This weekend, Suj is staying with my family in Otley for the weekend, so I hope my Under 9s play well for him.

In junior football, relatively small steps forward often represent major cause for celebration. I'm especially pleased that Suj is here to witness such an occasion today. Our opponents, Shipley, won all four games against us last year very easily. In one match they won 6-1. This morning, I was hoping for a big improvement, but as Shipley sped into a 2-0 lead, I sort of feared the worst. Last season, whenever we went one or two goals down, we just caved in and lost by a lot. Today, a penalty, given in dubious fashion it has to be said, saw the impressive Max Milner pull a goal back for us. Suddenly, my lads began believing in themselves and started playing like demons. Jack Wood equalised and the game was up for grabs. In the second half, Shipley regained the lead, before Matthew McGlinchey scored a great individual third for us. With most of the pressure on our defence, I kind of hoped we'd hold out for a draw at the very least. But with only minutes to go, Jimmy was unable to hold onto a long punt forward and from the rebound Shipley scored the winner.

When the final whistle went, I felt disappointment for myself and the boys, but knew at the same time that their performance signalled real progress. So, as always, after both sides had shaken hands on a great game, I got the boys together and told them they had every reason to feel pleased.

The B team though were less organised and despite being level at

1-1 for much of the first half, went on to concede another five without reply, confirming there is still a bit to do with these lads. Maybe I need to be more settled on formation and team selection. I have been chopping and changing a lot lately.

Monday 11th October.

Another day off work. This time to go walking with Suj in the Yorkshire Dales. We walk all morning, passing hundreds of sleepy rabbits, bathing in the sunshine of the river bank. By 12.30pm, we're in Appletreewick drinking a couple of pints of beer with lunch and at this point I feel like a long nap.

By the time we've walked back, it's mid-afternoon and Suj has to catch a train back to London. I drop him off at Guiseley station and head for home. Then I gather up the training kit, etc. and head off to Prince Henry's, with Jimmy, for training. I am early again, which gives me more time to do things. However, there are twenty-seven boys at training this week - a new record! We work on passing in relays and then do some heading. A feature in games so far this season has been the reluctance of some boys to head the ball, especially when coming down from a great height. This is even more prevalent in the Under 8 matches, according to Peter Smith. Some boys, like Sam Richmond - the smallest boy of the two age groups - are so shy of the ball they barely make contact with it. After a quick demonstration and a word or two of encouragement though, Sam's a changed lad, heading full on the forehead with eyes on the ball. More progress.

Wednesday 13th October.

I've booked myself on an F.A. Coaching session in Warrington on 1st November. Unfortunately, this will clash with a training session at Prince Henry's, so I'll have to ask Steve Milner and Peter Smith to help out in my absence.

Saturday 16th October.

There's been an earthquake in California with some people in Los

Angeles thrown out of their beds by the force. There are no serious casualties. My brothers live in San Diego, where they also felt the effect. When my mother phones to check they are alright, Paul has just got up and is having breakfast.
Paul: "Hello mother, nice of you to call."
Mum: "Did you sleep well dear?"
Paul: "Well, you know me mother, two hours at most, if I'm lucky."
(He supposedly suffers from insomnia.)
Mum: "You do realise there's been an earthquake don't you?"
Paul: "Has there? I'll turn the telly on."
My other brother, Dave, was still asleep in bed! Still, it's good to know they're OK I miss not seeing them, though I know they're having a great time coaching football to the American kids.

When we were young, it seemed like we played football together all the time. After school, in the evenings, at weekends, during the holidays. We'd even play on Christmas Day. That became a tradition. We played 2 v 1, 3-and-you're-in, 'cupies,' penalties, 'wallies.' Anything that involved kicking a ball. I was usually Alan Ball (I had the white boots), Dave was Joe Royle (he has me to thank for being another Everton fan) and Paul was George Best (he became a Red). In the local parks, we'd take on allcomers. We developed an almost telepathic understanding of how each other played. Instinctively, one would know where the other was running and what he'd do next. Years later, long after I'd left home, we would play together in matches and the same understanding remained. And in all the kick-about games we played together as kids, we only ever lost once. And that was playing against a team with an extra player.

In a way, small-sided football - what my junior teams play now - is the closest thing to those impromptu games played on back streets and parks everywhere, before the days of Game Boys and computers.

Tonight there's a message on the phone to say Matthew McGlinchey can't play tomorrow. Michael and Murray are unavailable too, so I hope no one else drops out, as I haven't any subs.

Sunday 17th October.
Away to Burley.

9.45am at Otley Town Football Club. All boys playing in the A team are meeting here, unless they're going straight to Burley. Matthew Waring, James Dalby and Max Milner are on time and we travel in convoy to the pitch. David Crane, the Burley manager is among a few putting up nets and marking out the pitch. We say hello and I notice straightaway that the grass is very long. The lads who are here now include Jack Wood, so only Andrew Kendall and Chris Baker are missing. It's still early. At 10.15am, my eldest son Joe runs on to the pitch where we're warming up to let me know that Chris Baker can't play and therefore isn't coming. Now I only have six players and that's if Andrew Kendall turns up. He isn't yet here, so I run over to Peter Smith, who's team are on the opposite pitch and about to play against Burley's Under 8s. He has a mobile phone, so I quickly give Julie Brotherton a call to see if Sean can get here early and play in goal. Fortunately, they're in and will set off shortly. Meanwhile, David Smith, who's not due to arrive until 11.00am turns up and as Andrew still isn't here, is instantly promoted to the starting line up of the A team.

Eventually, Sean arrives, dons the gloves and we kick-off just ten minutes late.

The long grass and the changes in personnel make for a more even game than I originally anticipated. Matthew Waring scores just on the stroke of half-time with a crisply struck shot, but in the second half, he unluckily deflects the ball past Sean to give Burley an equaliser. Despite missing one or two chances, we win it with a brilliant team goal. Good defending clears the ball to Jack, who runs into the opposition half, before switching play from right to left with a great cross-field pass. James, unmarked in front of goal can't miss.

In the B match, Sean turns striker and has a field day, scoring six times. He could have had more, but I decide to take him off for a while and give new boy Brendan Sutherland a game. He is one of a few lads who's been training most weeks, without so far competing in a match. Another is Andrew Newlove, who scores, as does Andrew Jefferies, Lloyd Almond and Adam Walker. One of the few boys not to score is Toby, who I eventually take off. I gently tease him about it, watching him pull his usual grumpy bottom lip out. His mum, Bev, laughs telling me not to be so mean. I put him back on and within a minute he races through the Burley defence with the ball, before shooting just wide with only the keeper to beat. I had to smile. It finishes 10-0. Our biggest ever win. I'm pleased for all of them, if not a little sorry for the Burley lads, some of whom clearly haven't played much football before.

The Under 8s also win, though I don't get chance to see them play.

With the matches over, I dash back home, drop off Jimmy, pick up Joe and drive down to his game eating on a piece of toast for my lunch.

Monday 18th October.

The biggest headache I've got at the moment is team selection on match days. Sometimes I agonise over who will play in what team and spend ages deciding. Writing boys' names down on bits of paper and then crossing them out again. Certainly, there are a core of lads who pick themselves - like Max, the two Matthews and Jack. Thereafter, Jimmy is probably the best goalkeeper, while Michael's speed and finishing usually gets him the nod. Murray is a clever player and James, extremely promising. Toby can be good when he wants to be and Sean scores goals, providing the opposition aren't too quick. Chris is intelligent and positions himself well on the field. He can also play in goal. Lloyd isn't strong when competing for the ball, but is pretty handy running with it. Andrew Kendall could be a good player, though at the moment, his lack of concentration and diminutive size often go against him. Adam and Callum, as beginners could do well, though it's early days. The other six? I'm not sure yet. What I do know is they all add up to twenty-one boys and twenty-one into two seven-a-side teams means not all of them can play at the same time. One substitute per team is OK, two is harder to accommodate when matches are only twenty minutes each way. But I do feel guilty leaving boys out. You can tell they're disappointed and I genuinely feel for them. There's nothing worse than when you want to play and your mates are and you know that they know you're not. It takes me back to my school days at break time, when the two best players picked the sides. Everyone had to line up, whilst the captains chose their teams: one man each until no one was left. And if you were one of the last to get picked, you felt like everyone was looking at you thinking you were useless, even if you knew you weren't. Which was tough.

Three lads still haven't played a match at all yet. Two only played for the first time at Burley. So what to do? All the lads can't be involved every week and I do want to develop two good sides. Maybe I'll rotate those on the fringes of the teams. Or maybe I'll try to arrange the occasional third team fixture as a friendly.

Turning with the ball is the theme for training tonight. Hook turns, instep turns, stop turns. Dribble, turn, pass. Building up the speed when they're confident enough with the technique.

With it being half-term, there are no games this weekend and no training session next Monday, as the school is closed. However, as I'm taking days off work during the holiday, I've arranged a outdoor practice at Otley Town on Thursday morning.

Sunday 24th October.

A rare Sunday off from football. There are no matches except the game in our garden. It's England versus Brazil. Jimmy is Taffarel, Brazil's goalkeeper. Joe is Alan Shearer and I'm Kevin Campbell - Everton's new super hero, suddenly elevated to the international stage. Campbell is magnificent, despite being rather tired after playing for Otley Town Reserves yesterday. He scores a hat-trick within a couple of minutes, despite Taffarel's outrageous and courageous diving about. Shearer's having a good game too, but he gets more than a little irritated when Campbell eventually lopes off inside for a cup of tea and Channel 4's TV coverage of the Milan derby.

Thursday 28th October.

Julie has gone to London for a break from the norm. Norm for me is another training session on a lovely sunny morning. A chance to put up the portable goals in preparation for some shooting. Norm is running about with enthusiasm, showing the boys how to warm up properly. How to stretch. How to shoot and how to volley. Norm is all about letting the boys play football when the coaching time is over. Norm is getting dirty and not caring. Norm is giving out teamsheets for the games on Sunday. Norm is packing up the balls, the markers and today, the goals. Norm is wondering whether the teams will play well and win this Sunday. Norm is great. Roll on more norm.

Friday 29th October.

My daughter, Maisie hates football. Her idea of fun is ballet dancing and gymnastics, which she's rather good at. But today, she has a new football friend, 'Scarfy'. Scarfy is a six foot long, blue and white knitted Everton scarf that I've had since I was ten years old. I've just re-discovered it in the loft and whilst Jimmy and Joe claim the pennants and other silk scarfs (mementoes from various cup finals), Maisie likes the woollen one best. Tonight, she is sitting up in bed reading a story to Scarfy. Scarfy is listening, propped up on his own pillow, on his side of the bed. He is obviously enjoying the story very much. Albert Einstein once said, *"Imagination is more important than knowledge."* I'll go along with that.

Sunday 31st October.
Away to Oakworth and Silsden.

Halloween Horrors (Part One):
1. Getting up at 7.45am on a Sunday morning. 2. Driving all the way to Oakworth - a twenty-five minute journey - to find I've only got six players. 3. Standing around on a wild and windy football pitch, with the opposition ready, trying to delay the kick-off in the hope that one of my two other lads makes it in time. (Fortunately, Chris does.) 4. Having to constantly shout at Lloyd Almond to get back in defence, as, for the umpteenth time, Oakworth attack without any help for our lone defender, Jimmy. (Despite all this, the B team play quite well and win 3-2. Matthew M and Murray (2), getting the goals.)

Halloween Horrors (Part Two):
1. Getting back to Otley at 11.15am and leaving again for the A team match at 11.20am. 2. Getting stuck in heavy traffic on the only major road out of Otley to Silsden. 3. Trying to take the scenic route and realising too late that the rest of the world has done the same. 4. Getting no reply, when at 12.30pm I phone the number of the Silsden manager, Paul Smith, to explain we might not make the game. 5. Finally arriving half an hour late, at 1.00pm and having to kick-off straightaway. 6. Watching a game I thought we'd win, end in a draw. Even a wonder goal from Max Milner - a half-volley lob from distance into the top corner of the net - can't disguise an overall feeling of disappointment.

Jimmy Garner Currie

Otley Town Juniors Under 9s
Date of Birth: 9th July 1991
Position: Goalkeeper or defender
Nickname: Bob
Favourite football team: Everton
Favourite food: Woolies Pick 'n Mix
Favourite drink: Pepsi
Best thing outside football:
My gun that fires foam bullets
What I'll be when I'm grown up:
A footballer

*****

JIMMY GARNER CURRIE
OTLEY TOWN JUNIORS — GOALKEEPER

ANDREW KENDALL
OTLEY TOWN JUNIORS — DEFENDER

Andrew Kendall

Otley Town Juniors Under 9s
Date of Birth: *12th June 1991*
Position: *Defender*
Nickname: *Razor*
Favourite football team: *Leeds Utd*
Favourite food: *Pizza*
Favourite drink: *Dr Pepper*
Best thing outside football:
Playing on my Game Boy
What I'll be when I'm grown up:
A footballer

*****

NOVEMBER

Monday 1st November.

I feel like punching myself tonight. I've taken the afternoon off work, to attend an F.A. Coaching Session at North Cheshire College in Warrington, but having set off too late to miss the rush hour, I'm stuck in heavy traffic on the M62. Fortunately, I just about make the 7.30pm session on time. Along with about sixty other football coaches, the gymnasium at the college is heaving and it's not easy to obtain a good view. Tonight's topic involves the Under 12 boys from Bolton Wanderers Youth Academy and the coaches running the session are ex-professional players, Chris Sulley and a guy whose name I didn't catch. The emphasis is on screening the ball correctly. This is practised by each individual boy, with and without an opponent. Chris makes the point that as a skill, screening is not practised nearly enough by our youngsters. Consequently, British professionals sometimes lack the technique that clubs on the continent, such as Ajax, perfect.

The set-ups are very well presented, in a gym slightly smaller than Prince Henry's in Otley. There are only nine players for Chris and his colleague to organise and each of the boys present is extremely talented, being able to use both feet very well. It is also clear that the boys are there to listen and learn, eager to impress and stay very much part of a professional football club set-up. Compare that to my upwards-of-thirty at training, with younger lads and bigger ability differences. Also, I rarely have the luxury of a trouble-free evening. There's always at least one boy messing about.

It's after 10.30pm when I eventually get home. (I wonder how Steve Milner and Peter Smith have got on, running the Under 9s training session without me.)

Friday 5th November.

A chance meeting with Ron Brown at the Clifton Village Bonfire. He lets me know that the Hawley family have moved out of the area. This means that young Alex has left and I'm sad to see him go. One of the funniest lads in my charge, he is also a fantastic dribbler and will surely make a good footballer. The same goes for his older brother, Jamie who was playing for the Under 10s. Both Hawleys were at my very first training session, back in July 1997 and I wish them well.

Sunday 7th November.
Home to Bingley.

The short journey from Clifton into Otley is more than familiar. After five years of living in the village, I feel I know it blindfold. Up the short narrow lane from our rented farmhouse, I drive past grazing cows and sheep, towards the giant candle-like TV mast. A 'blind' right-hand turn into the main road, takes me downhill and over the dip, where many a speedy driver has come a cropper, ending up in a cow-pat through a drystone wall. From here a marvellous view of Otley presents itself - especially breathtaking when skies are blue and a great cloud of mist hugs the valley. Today it's just grey. I pass the Spite pub and accelerate, before slowing by the ridiculous 'Welcome to Leeds' sign at the top of the steep Carr Bank. (The sign has been graffittied, obliterating the word 'Leeds' in favour of 'Otley.' The sentiment is spot on - Leeds city centre is a further fifteen or so miles away.) Down past the Wharfedale hospital, Prince Henry's school and the Otley cattle market. Over the bridge of the River Wharfe, turning left at The Cove Fish & Chip restaurant, so avoiding the town centre. Out on the Pool Road for half a mile, past Otley Rugby Club and Stephen Smith's Garden Centre, before indicating right up the short rough track to the football club - an annoying little roller-coaster ride, more often than not strewn with muddy brown puddles - and park in front of the clubhouse. There's no one else around. It is 8.45am.

By 10.00am, I have marked out the pitch and the place is filling up with people. The Under 13s are at home as well as my Under 9s, so there are vehicles a plenty in the car park. Steve Milner and Rod Almond help me put up the nets and by 10.30am, the A team have kicked off against Bingley. By 10.31am, they're a goal up and I sense a good day. Matthew M adds a well deserved hat-trick to Murray's opener and in a highly entertaining and competitive match, they win 4-2. Unfortunately, the B team lose by the same score, despite a couple of goals by Sean Brotherton.

It's a sign of growing expectations when one or two parents observe after today's game that the boys haven't played quite as well as in previous matches. Last season, the A team had to play out of their skin to win at all. This season, we can win without being at our best. The A team record so far is: played 10, won 6, drawn 1, lost three. Goals for 38, goals against 22. Not quite up to championship form, but we are becoming harder to beat. (Am I sounding like Match of the Day pundit Alan Hansen?)

Monday 8th November.

Black Monday. A very difficult evening starts with the Under 15s believing that they should be in the gym instead of us. Despite the fact that we've been inside since the end of September and that I was given the 6.30pm - 7.30pm slot at an August managers' meeting, the Under 15s manager, Chip, is none too happy. His lot have been at Otley Town on Tuesdays and Thursdays training outside, until tonight. Now they suddenly decide to come indoors. Chip was apparently told by Malcolm Dobinson that the gym was free, which can only mean I dreamt about the managers' meeting on Monday 2nd August, when all the gym allocations were discussed. And I must have been talking to myself when, having had Mondays at 6.30pm offered to me, I'd said "yes." And nobody objected. It's very frustrating to have to stand and argue about it, when all the boys - bored of waiting - are charging about the place kicking balls everywhere and making a tremendous racket. I tell Chip I'm not going anywhere and make a mental note to take up the issue with Malcolm later.

With the night off to a bad start and twenty-nine crazed lads to sort out, things get worse before they get better. The first half-hour is chaotic and I am forced to abandon my original plan in favour of small-sided games of football. By this time, the Under 8s have gone, which helps the numbers somewhat. I introduce a condition during the games, that one boy must play 'the sweeper role' (in other words, stay in his own half at all times). This helps the boys to spread out more and stops their natural tendency to bunch around the ball.

Two new boys have joined us tonight from Weston Lane Juniors. Josh Waite, in particular, is exceptional for his age and will be good news for the A team. He seems to know a lot of the other boys - Max, Jack, Adam, Callum and Louis all go to the same junior school. And they all want to be on his side when the games start, so he's instantly popular. (I remember him for the goal he scored against us back in August!) His dad, Phil, a footballer himself, has offered to help at training. The other boy, Tom Sellars, is also a good player, though he's not available for matches as he prefers playing rugby.

Thursday 11th November.

For the fifth night in a row, I'm on the phone trying to make contact with the manager of Idle Saints, who the A team are playing this Sunday. As it is the 'home' managers' prerogative to fix the times of matches, I've already organised them from my end,

35

as well as handing teamsheets to all my boys' parents. The A match is fixed for 10.30am with the B team playing Cullingworth at 11.30am. Unfortunately for me, the name of the Idle manager and his telephone number are wrong in the League Handbook. I am thus sent on a ring-a-ring-merry-go-round from Sunday night to finally get my man tonight. And the first thing he tells me is that as a church-going side, Idle don't play on a Sunday morning. This means another round of ring-a-ring-ring contacting all my parents, and changing the kick-off to 1.15pm. Fortunately, all the boys, except Murray, can play at the revised time. Murray will have to play for the B team this week.

Saturday 13th November.

On the eve of a busy morning, with everything finally sorted, Toby's mum, Bev phones to tell me her son can't play tomorrow as he's 'grounded' for being naughty at school. And Lynne Kendall calls to tell me that Andrew has been throwing up and is therefore not fit. To complete the misery, Malcolm rings to tell me he's given the training time slot for the Under 8s (5.30-6.30pm) to Chip and the Under 15s. My Under 9s will still have the 6.30-7.30pm slot, but I won't now be able to coach the Under 8s. Peter Smith is now very angry, feeling extremely let down, which makes me feel bad. Whatever happened to football being fun?

Sunday 14th November. Home to Cullingworth and Idle Saints.

9.30am on a cold, damp morning. Having dropped my eldest son, Joe off at the Lix carpark for his game with the Under 12s and feeling guilty that again, I can't watch him, I head for the Club. There is no line marker. I stomp about angrily wondering where it is, before someone reckons he saw Ron Brown take it up to Wharfemeadow Fields. I get in my car, slamming the door and drive faster than I should to the other side of Otley. Parking as near as I can to the pitch, I slither down the muddy bank to the place where Ron's Under 11s are playing. Fortunately he has finished with the marker, so I grab it and start pushing it back up the slope to my car. Unfortunately, it is very heavy and too slippy a bank to get up easily. I lose my temper and tip all the lime out on the pathway, covering myself in the process. Cursing under my breath, I charge back to my car, bundle the cumbersome marker into the boot and hurtle back to the club.

By the time the boys arrive for the matches, I have calmed down. John Hutchinson has arrived to take pictures and what a game he sees! The B team, 4-1 down at one stage, come back in the second half to win an incredible match, 7-5. Debutant, Josh Waite scores five times and is the main reason we turn the game round. Murray and Lloyd get the other goals.

Afterwards, there is a specially arranged C team match against Cullingworth B for all those boys who rarely play. In contrast to the previous encounter, the football is slower and largely uneventful. However, boys such as Simon and Brendan seem to enjoy it and I'm glad to provide a match for them. We go down by two goals to nil.

Finally, on a pitch that is now all but mud, the A team win comfortably against the church-going Idle Saints, 6-0. Matthew McGlinchey scores twice, with the other goals coming from Matthew Waring, Max, Jack and James.

At the end of it all, it is way after two o'clock, I am cold and my right leg is increasingly sore. (Yet another injury.) When I get home, I sit down with a nice hot cup of tea and watch

T.V. - an ice-pack on what is probably a torn muscle in my calf. Peter Smith phones in the evening to see how we got on and says he has spoken to Malcom, who apparently, now blames me for the training fiasco. Oh bliss and joy.

Monday 15th November.

Saturday 5th July, 1997 seems a long, long time ago. It was my very first coaching session and I don't remember much about it, except I know I had a plan. I went over and over that plan in my mind, making sure I knew the practice inside out and even rehearsing the words I would use to explain myself. I was in the process of taking my F.A. Coaching Certificate and the motto I had impregnated on my brain was, *"If you fail to prepare, then prepare to fail."*

I had already done a few sessions with my colleagues on the Course, as well as the odd hour or so coaching two older age groups from Otley Town Juniors, but this was the 'Big One' - my first time with boys I would coach every week. I had no idea how it would go or whether I'd really be any good at it. I do remember getting down to Prince Henry's playing fields early that morning, marking out the practice area with cones and trying to imagine if the spaces would fit the boys and ideas I had on paper.

Of those sixteen boys, on that fine summer morning, seven - Jimmy, Jack, Max, Chris, Lloyd, David and Andrew Kendall - still play for the Under 9s, whilst another four - Arran, Stuart, Charlie and Joshua play for the Under 8s. (Alex and Jamie Hawley were also there, but have now moved on.)

Tonight is the 100th training session with my lads. The significance of the occasion would probably be lost on them, so I keep the moment to myself. There are no Under 8s tonight, as their coaching session has moved to Wednesdays. It's a shame the way all that happened, but less boys in the gym does make my job a lot easier.

Thursday 18th November.

Headlines in the sports pages of the Wharfedale Observer highlight the demise of the cricket section at Otley Town. Whilst this is sad for the cricket lovers, my mind races, anticipating a football club with a larger playing area and my Under 9s knocking it about 'Brazil style' on the cricket square. (We'll have to wait and see!)

Friday 19th November.

My brother Paul has broken his foot and I know instantly how down and frustrated he must be feeling, having broken bones myself in the past. The first realisation - after the initial pain has subsided - is that you can't play football. I remember breaking my right leg in a match in London in 1988. Whilst the pain was horrendous - two canisters of gas and air on the way to Ealing Hospital only numbing the inevitable agony later - what really hurt was the frustration of hobbling around on crutches for months afterwards. The boredom of days watching Laverne and Shirley on TV, listening to the Tony Blackburn Radio Show and figuring out how to manoeuvre a cup of tea from one room to another. The days without football and the frightening sight of what was left of my leg, when it was removed from plaster.

Sunday 21st November.
Away to Shelf and Wilsden.

I leave the house at 9.15am and drive down to the club with Jimmy for a 9.30am meet. It is a cold and frosty morning and the ground is hard under foot. Hopefully, the pitch at Shelf won't be frozen. We travel in a convoy of cars to the Halifax side of Bradford, which takes slightly less than half an hour. When we arrive, I quickly change into my boots and give the boys a warm-up in anticipation of a close game. Shelf have the same number of league points as us, whilst we also had a close game with them at the Otley 6-a-side Tournament last season. However, with what probably amounts to my strongest side, we win comfortably 4-1. New lad, Josh, contributes much to a fine team performance. He scores twice, Max gets a penalty and Matthew McGlinchey the other. After the match, the Shelf manager, Richard Hartley, generously remarks on how well we pass the ball around as a team - a comment which leaves me feeling well satisfied.

My dad, who's come along to watch, then takes Jimmy home, whilst I drive off towards Wilsden for the B and C team matches. I have a bit of time to kill, so I stop off at McDonald's for a cup of tea and a burger, jotting down notes for the match report later.

The early part of the afternoon is all about Toby Hall. The bad boy made good. The boy who couldn't play last week on account of being naughty. Seven days of early to bed seem to have re-energised a lad who rarely smiles, but is a lad I have a lot of time for. Today as goalkeeper for the B team, he performs heroically, making more saves in one match than most keepers do in ten. Losing 3-0 is a minor miracle. But for Toby, it could have been double figures. The B team should have done better and to compound it all, Michael Beecroft even misses a penalty.

Andrew Newlove hasn't turned up, so the C team are a man short. With the day becoming distinctly colder, Bev Beecroft, in particular, looks less than delighted her son Michael wants to play in another match. He makes it all worthwhile, I'm sure, with the only goal of a fairly even encounter, making amends for his miss in the previous game. And apart from spending five minutes, wandering around the pitch, looking for a missing ball, it is a worthwhile exercise for me, giving boys like David Smith, Simon Harris, Andrew Jefferies and Brendan Sutherland, all regular attendees at training sessions, an opportunity to play a match. Though I would be over-stretching myself to arrange three matches every week, I don't mind doing it on an occasional basis. Nevertheless, it is a welcome sight to be arriving home again at 3.15pm. For once, I've had enough of football for one day.

Monday 22nd November.

After yesterday's long haul, the thought of training the boys seems a mighty imposition tonight. But at 6.30pm, twenty eager, bouncing boys entering the gym have an invigorating effect on me and within minutes, I am nine years old again.

Sunday 28th November. Away to Nab Wood.

Today is all about the Vanishing White Cardboard Box. It's a container that holds some photographs John Hutch has taken of the lads from the Under 8s, some training bibs and an allocation of raffle tickets. All the contents I am entrusted to hand over to Peter Smith. When I arrive at the club for our early morning meet with the boys and parents travelling to Nab Wood, Peter is struggling to assemble a new set of junior goals. I put the White Box down on some breeze blocks and help him out for a few minutes.....

At Nab Wood, it is very windy and the pitch has a slope. I have my daughter Maisie with me today and she's none too happy having to watch football, so bringing the flask of hot chocolate is a bright idea. It keeps her warm at least.

I am expecting both teams to win comfortably, though you never can tell with boys. The A Team exceed expectations. Performance-wise, they pass the ball brilliantly and are soon well on top. After the fourth goal goes in, two of their lads start fighting among themselves. My boys don't quite know how to behave. On the one hand, they're celebrating a goal and on the other, half laughing and half embarrassed by the antics in front of them. To give credit to the Nab Wood manager, he drags off the main culprit and I don't think he gets back on the pitch again. In the end we dish out a 9-1 thrashing with the goal-scorers, Josh (2), Matthew M (3),

Jack (2), Toby and Matthew W.

The wind really gets up for the second game and the B Team struggle a bit. In hindsight I regret not mixing up the two teams more. Michael scores twice, but we have to make do with a draw.

Later that afternoon, I remember the White Cardboard Box and call Peter Smith at home. "What box?" he says, as I hopefully inquire as to whether he noticed it or not. And despite a trip back to the club and a lot of ringing round, no one else has seen it either. The White Cardboard Box is never seen again.

Monday 29th November.

I'm not really sure how good a football coach I really am. My biggest fear is becoming the sort of manager that Alex Stock refers to in his 1982 book, 'A little thing called Pride.' *"Everywhere I go there are coaches. Schoolmasters telling young boys not to do this and not to do that and generally scaring the life out of the poor little devils. Junior clubs playing with sweepers, one and a half men up front, no wingers, four across the middle. They are frightened to death of losing, even at their tender age and it makes me cry."*

I took my F.A. Coaching Certificate because I wanted to coach boys the right way. The course was one of the most exhausting experiences of my life, both mentally and physically. I lost count of the hours that got me the badge. And though I loved every minute, when it was over, I breathed a great sigh of relief. It was a lot like passing my driving test. But as every driver knows, passing is only the start. So I find myself now, analysing whether shouting instructions from the touchline during matches - albeit in a positive manner - constitutes good or bad coaching. Should a good coach save all his talking for the training ground and stay silent during games, so as not to confuse or put undue pressure on young minds? Or can being vocally enthusiastic be helpful? During my coaching course, I was criticised for 'commentating' or talking too much from the touchline. It is something I try to keep to a minimum, but in the heat of a match, I become a player, a manager, a dad and a supporter, all rolled into one. The cool, calm, overseeing coach often gets lost in the passion of it all.

Tonight, as a direct consequence of these thoughts, the training session incorporates passing, control and turning with the ball. Boys working in threes, with an emphasis on giving each other information. In other words, asking them to talk. It never ceases to amaze me how much noise twenty boys can make in a gym when they're mucking about, but put them in a game situation and they're all as quiet as mice. Perhaps if they all start organising themselves during matches, I won't have to say a dicky bird.

Callum Shaw

Otley Town Juniors Under 9s
Date of Birth: *30th November 1990*
Position: *Defender*
Nickname: *None*
Favourite football team: *Leeds Utd*
Favourite food: *Burger & chips*
Favourite drink: *Cola*
Best thing outside football:
My Playstation
What I'll be when I'm grown up:
A footballer or a pilot

★ ★ ★ ★ ★

CALLUM SHAW
OTLEY TOWN JUNIORS — DEFENDER

Josh Waite

Otley Town Juniors Under 9s
Date of Birth: *10th October 1990*
Position: *Midfield*
Nickname: *Waitey*
Favourite football team: *Leeds Utd*
Favourite food: *Pasta*
Favourite drink: *Dr Pepper*
Best thing outside football:
Playing basketball
What I'll be when I'm grown up:
A footballer

★ ★ ★ ★ ★

JOSH WAITE
OTLEY TOWN JUNIORS — MIDFIELD

DECEMBER

Friday 3rd December.

At work today I get a call from a guy called Steve Eley at Aireborough Sports Centre in Guiseley. He asks if I'd be interested in a paid coaching position on Saturday mornings from January next year. He explains about the areas' Striker Awards Scheme, which is basically a soccer skills programme for children from the age of five. It began as an initiative of John Conway and John Hall at the Leeds Coaches Association and it was they who passed my name on to Steve. I'm definitely interested, but ask for some time to consider the position. We agree I'll phone with an answer next week.

Saturday 4th December.

A miserable day. Heavy snowfall almost puts paid to my own chances of playing for Otley Town today. We do though and lose heavily, as do Everton to Manchester United. (They've now gone eight games without a win and slipped to 12th in the league.) To complete a grim afternoon, I also aggravate a groin injury. When I get home, I'm in a bad mood. This is made worse when I get the message that Bolton Woods can't make the Under 9s fixture tomorrow. Bloody great. Wearily, I phone round all of the parents, breaking the news. Jimmy is disappointed the match is off, but on the bright side, I can now watch Joe play instead.

Sunday 5th December.

Following a heavy frost overnight, Joe's match is called off. Now Joe is disappointed, I'm disappointed and my dad, who's staying over for the weekend, is disappointed. It reminds me much of last season, when lots of matches were either cancelled or postponed due to bad weather. At the end of last season, I wrote a letter to Eddie Presland, the organiser of the Norman Bairstow League, suggesting that he incorporate a midwinter break. This year it's happened, which is sensible. It also gives everyone a rest and takes away the purgatory of turning out in severe weather. As much as I love the sport, I'm still haunted by memories of freezing cold days, playing school football on Townley playing fields in Burnley. Hands red raw and feet like blocks of ice. Unable to untie boot laces, I often felt like crying. And that horrible, tingling, burning sensation, stood in the hot showers afterwards, as my frozen body tried to get warm again. My lads don't need that.

Monday 6th December.

Rush, rush, rush. Why is there never enough time in the day? I'm late leaving work tonight, which always winds me up, especially when I've got to be somewhere for a certain time. I don't like to be late. When I finally get to Prince Henry's I get the impression the boys have been there ages, waiting. Several of them - Adam, Louis and Sean, are always early, which is good really and it shows they love coming. The boys cheer loudly as I struggle in with all the balls and markers - probably as much in relief that a ball to kick has arrived.

Last season, when we were forced to train in the cramped Chippendale School gym, there was one particular evening when everything seemed to go wrong. As tonight, I was late due to working commitments. And because I still had work to go back to, I arrived hoping my two regular helpers - Steve Milner and Paul Danskin - would be able to take over, allowing me to leave the session early. Neither were there of course, both working themselves. So I stayed as long as I dared, before asking parents, Bev Beecroft and Steve Jefferies, if they wouldn't mind rescuing the situation. I flew off in my car, back to work, feeling guilty, only to discover later that the moment I'd gone, the only ball I'd left them with had burst.

Straight after training tonight, it's the monthly junior managers meeting, at the Summercross pub, in Otley. It turns out to be a long evening. Major changes within the club are discussed, including the withdrawal of the cricket section, as disclosed in the newspaper last week. The meeting finishes at 11.30pm and I get home just before midnight. I've had no tea.

Wednesday 8th December.

After meeting Steve Eley in Guiseley at the sports centre, I decide to accept the offer of football coach at Aireborough. He seems a nice guy and I think it's an opportunity to add much to my experience, if not to my bank balance. I'll be coaching two groups of Under 7s between 9am and 11am on Saturdays, starting the second week in January.

Saturday 11th December.

I confirm the matches for tomorrow, despite the wet weather. I also arrange for someone to open the clubhouse, so parents and boys can have a get-together after the football is over. These will be the last fixtures before Christmas and the mid-winter break. In lots of ways, I'm all but ready for a rest and a battery re-charge.

Sunday 12th December.
Home to Burley and Ilkley.

This morning, I'm up at 7.45am and at the club an hour later. The ground is heavy with water, but just about playable. Anyway, given the amount of organisation, I have no intention of calling it off.

Peter Smith and I mark out two pitches on ground least affected by weather. Richard Danskin turns up to help, as his Under 12s fixture has been postponed. (Joe is unhappy for the second week running.) Suddenly, a multitude of hands are at the ready - Steve Milner and Steve Jefferies arrive - and all is sorted by ten o'clock. All the boys, bar Toby Hall, have turned up, so the games commence. Peter's Under 8s play Ilkley Under 8s on one pitch, whilst my B Team play Burley's A Team on the other. After those games, the A Team play Ilkley Under 9s and the C Team play Burley's B Team.

Afterwards, I need a drink and a sandwich, which are provided for in the bar. We reflect on the close game the Under 8s had and how the Under 9s B Team almost rescued a 0-5 scoreline to finish 3-5 (Michael scoring twice and Sean the other). The C Team, under the charge of Steve Jefferies, unfortunately lose 10-1 (Lloyd scoring), whilst the A Team register their biggest ever win, by 13-0 (goals from Max with a penalty, Matthew McGlinchey (2), Josh (2), Matthew Waring, James, an own goal and Jack Wood gets 5!)

Monday 13th December.

The last training session of the century. Nineteen of twenty-three boys are present. By way of a change tonight, I begin the evening by telling the boys a funny story. It involves a man on his way to the train station, when "full of wind," he succeeds in soiling his pants and trousers. More than a touch distressed, he heads for Marks & Spencer to buy a new pair of underpants and trousers. With the goods in the bag, he runs to the station and hops on the train, just as it's pulling out of the platform. He makes his way to the sanctuary of the toilet, removes the dirty items and throws them out of the window. Free from the embarrassing evidence and smell, the man reaches into his Marks & Spencer's carrier, only to discover a cardigan and the slow realisation that he's picked up the wrong bag from the shop!

Now whether this story is true or not, it had the boys more captivated than any football technique I've tried to teach them, this season or last. Perhaps there's a lesson there somewhere.

After that bit of nonsense, I set up some shooting practice, which they all really enjoy, to the point where we almost run out of time to play small-sided games.

Training over, I give each of the lads a chocolate selection box by way of a Christmas present and wish them and their parents a good and enjoyable holiday.

Saturday 18th December.

At long last. Everton's first victory in ten matches. OK it's only against lowly Watford, but a win's a win.

Friday 24th December.

The many-numbered Wood family come over for a pre-Christmas eat and drink. Joanne gives me a cute looking Otley Town footballer with my name on it. She's made it from salt dough and then painted and varnished it. Ha! It doesn't look a bit like me.

Sunday 26th December.

Boxing Day. Everton versus Sunderland at Goodison Park. And one of those great afternoons when all pre-match anxieties and gut-churning tensions disappear quickly under an avalanche of goals. I'm sitting at the Gladwys Street End scarcely believing the ease at which we destroy the opposition. Current form billed it as a could-go-either-way game, but Everton play Sunderland off the park and win 5-0. It could have been a lot more too, but this result has certainly made my Christmas.

Friday 31st December.

With the TV and radio on in various rooms in the house, it seems there is a different place in the world celebrating the Millennium on each and every hour of the day. At around 2pm, I finally give in to the persuasive powers of my children and take them down to the local park in Otley. Joe and I kick a ball around, whilst Jimmy and Maisie prefer a game of climbing along a wall, clinging to the railings.

Later, Peter Smith calls to wish me well and to relay a little story about his son Martin, who's been attending some football coaching sessions in Yeadon. The best bit occurred the day Martin got honoured with the informal "Player of the Day" award for his performance as a goalkeeper. The Coach, obviously knowing Martin as a character who likes to chatter, jokingly suggested a speech. True to form, he stood up, took the award and addressed all the players and watching parents: "On behalf of all goalkeepers everywhere........."

CHRISTOPHER BAKER
OTLEY TOWN JUNIORS — DEFENDER

Christopher Baker

Otley Town Juniors Under 9s
Date of Birth: *8th March 1991*
Position: *Defender or goalkeeper*
Nickname: *Dave*
Favourite football team: *Barnsley*
Favourite food: *Chicken dinner*
Favourite drink: *Lilt*
Best thing outside football:
Playing the piano
What I'll be when I'm grown up:
A footballer

* * * * *

Simon Harris

Otley Town Juniors Under 9s
Date of Birth: *19th September 1990*
Position: *Goalkeeper*
Nickname: *None*
Favourite football team: *Bradford*
Favourite food: *Tuna plate*
Favourite drink: *Fanta orange*
Best thing outside football:
Reading Harry Potter books
What I'll be when I'm grown up:
A footballer

* * * * *

SIMON HARRIS
OTLEY TOWN JUNIORS — GOALKEEPER

JANUARY

Saturday 1st January 2000.

At midnight, my family and I are celebrating the dawn of a new Millennium, with friends at a private party. Drinking champagne in time with many millions across the country, Clifton village offers a quite amazing and spectacular view of fireworks all along the Wharfe Valley.

At one o'clock, we walk the way home by torchlight. Up the country lane on tired legs, manager and son singing "Ten green bottles" and "One man went to mow." Good thing there's no game in the morning.

Saturday 8th January.

My first paid coaching session doing the Striker Awards. I'm at Aireborough before nine o'clock and everything is set up ready for me in the sports hall. I've got sixteen boys for the first hour session and another sixteen, from ten o'clock, for the second hour. It goes well, though getting to know that many new boys will take some time.

Everton are through to the 5th round of the F.A. Cup, after beating Birmingham City at home 2-0. Could we go all the way?

Monday 10th January.

The first session of a new year for the Otley Under 9s is a gentle one. A little work on passing and ball control and lots of time for games of football. It's interesting to sit back and watch them play. Certain boys are fast developing into cracking players. After Josh Waite, who is literally head and shoulders above the rest, Max Milner comes first to mind. One of 'the originals', Max came training when I started coaching the boys two years ago. He's a lad I've a lot of time for and he stood out then as one who listens and learns better than most. A natural defender given his size and strength, he is now realising when to get forward during games and have an influence in the opposition's half. His goal at Silsden in October, certainly emphasised that. Jack Wood (or 'Five' as I sometimes like to refer to him now), is also an 'original'. He, like Max, is a good listener and with his excellent technique, is often used as a model in training, to show other boys how to do something. Jack is an unselfish player and uses the ball more intelligently than anyone else. Both boys are a credit to their respective parents and should be proud of the way they conduct themselves.

In the evening, I write a letter to all of the parents informing them of my holiday to the United States. I'm going on a two week break to celebrate my 40th birthday with my brothers, who live in San Diego. Julie and my own parents are paying for the flight, which is fantastic of them. I fly, via Chicago, on Tuesday 25th January.

Sunday 16th January.

A little bit of a waste of time. With no organised matches, today was supposed to be an A Team versus B Team game, plus a friendly match against the Under 8s for the boys in the C Team. Unfortunately, not enough boys turn up, so it ends up as a small-sided game and penalty competition for those not involved in the match against Peter's boys.

Later, I finalise the arrangements for next Sunday's game against Bolton Woods, a team we've never beaten. The very first time I tried to speak to Steve Shackleton, their manager, his wife answered the phone. Or was it their dog? Come to think of it, their noisy kids were also on the line, including a crying baby. There was such a racket, God knows how I ever found out where their pitch was or the time of the kick off. To their credit, Steve and his wife gave me a lot of helpful steers when I was finding my feet in the early part of last season. And for that I'm very grateful. However, this time I'm making the arrangements.

" Steve?"

" Yeah."

" Mark Currie from Otley Town Juniors. Is ten thirty OK for the match this weekend? "

" Yeah."

" Right, fine."

And we have a chat about how each other's teams are getting on - only this time there are no dogs or crying babies.

Monday 17th January.

It's always strange when my own son, Jimmy is not at training. Not that he's missed many, but tonight there's a birthday party for him to go to. Jimmy was the whole reason I started the coaching thing in the first place and although after two years, I feel very attached to all of the other boys, my own son is obviously number one. Sometimes it can be difficult coaching him whilst also being his dad. I try to treat him like the rest, though there have been odd moments when he's put me in an awkward position - like the time he refused to join in the practice match at training last year. That particular night, he was all crazy and extremely unreasonable. Whilst all the other boys were waiting patiently for me to tell them what to do, Jimmy was this angry, emotional, highly-charged bomb exploding right in my face. What went on in his head is anyone's guess, but eventually he came round. I guess it's all about a level of maturity, because most of the time, he just gets on and enjoys himself, like the others. And though he isn't yet one of the better outfield players, he has a natural energy and enthusiasm that is just there in him. I didn't coach that and I don't think you can coach that. Every now and then though, I'd like to spend some quality time alone with him and with his older brother Joe to improve their technique. But by the time the coaching of the Under 9s is over and the matches are over and the Aireborough coaching is over and I've played myself, the clock's run down.

Sunday 23rd January.
Home to Bolton Woods.

We've played Bolton Woods about five times in all and lost the lot. Last year we went to their place without Max and lost 7-0. Today, I've a feeling we might just win, if we play well. But they're usually a strong team, so who knows?

It turns out to be one our best performances so far this season. We start well, with lots of early pressure, but then Jimmy has to pull off a great double save to keep us in the game. Then the flood gates open. Amazingly, we're 3-0 up by half-time. Matthew McGlinchey and Murray Simm combine brilliantly together, score a goal apiece and lay one on for Josh. Although Bolton Woods don't seem quite as strong as last year, we're passing the ball around and playing really well. The second half, we're totally on top, although they hit the woodwork three times. Josh gets a hat-trick, Matthew M ends up with four, Murray gets another and even substitute David Smith scores. Right at the end, Bolton Woods finally get a consolation goal, to much ironic and relieved cheering from the visiting parents.

I have some mixed feelings about winning by so many goals. On the one hand it's great for my boys to win 10-1, but despite the fact they they stuffed us last year, I do feel sorry for the opposition. I could feel and understand the frustration of their coach, Steve Shackleton, on the opposite touchline.

The B team game is much closer, though we win 3-1. James, Sean and Michael getting the goals - the latter, a great shot direct from a free kick. So I feel pretty good today. And not a bad way to go off for a two week holiday.

Monday 24th January.

The last session before flying to the States. Tonight, I highlight how well all the boys played yesterday and reflect in particular, on the goal that Sean Brotherton scored for the B Team. The way he moved off the ball to receive a pass from James, before scoring in the corner. It was great stuff. I bring out Sean in front of the rest to re-live the move and to help make my point. Sean falls over the ball, ending up in a heap on the floor, so I smile and move on.

After the session, I give all the football gear to Steve Milner, who's taking over the boys in my absence with Josh Waite's dad, Phil. I give Steve the teamsheets for the next two weeks and the league booklet, my folder and attendance book. Bev Beecroft gives me a bottle of champagne, whilst a couple of the boys give me cards - Chris and Jack - who's turned up despite being too unwell to train.

It seems strange to arrive home without all the cumbersome balls, cones and bags. I quickly change out of my training gear and pack my suitcase. Saying goodbye to Julie and the children seems odd too. The whole idea of a holiday without them, somehow unreal. We say our farewells and then I'm away to my mum's house, near Burnley, where I'll stay the night, before being taken to Manchester airport by my dad in the morning.

Wednesday 26th January.

It's a busman's holiday already. My first full day in America and I'm coaching football, or soccer, as they refer to it here. Both my brothers coach professionally in California for a junior club called the Del Mar Sharks. The climate is good all year round in San Diego, so it encourages an almost seasonless activity. I'm helping my brother Paul coach three Indian children in a private session. It's not a bad hour and a half either. Not only is it warm and sunny, but Paul pays me half of his fifty dollars earnings. Paul and Dave both do a regular amount of private or personal coaching, which supplements the salaries paid by the club for the team sessions, matches and tournaments. Being English and knowing football is a useful commodity in the States and both my brothers are taking full advantage. Now, how can I persuade Julie to come and live out here?

Thursday 27th January.

This afternoon, I'm helping my younger brother, Dave, coach his Under 10 girls team. This would be unusual in England, but here, football is as popular with girls as it is with boys. And most of them are pretty good. Dave has them well-drilled and is not afraid to get tough with them, if they do something wrong. This would be slightly contrary to my methods back home, but here it is different. Firstly, the players' parents expect Dave to get results because they pay for the privilege. And also because the American kids are constantly being told how great they are by their peers, they often need to be brought down to earth a bit.

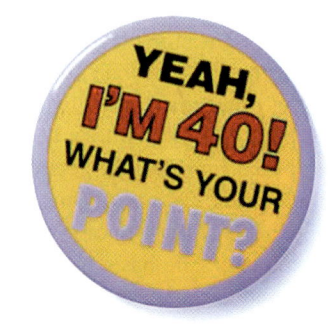

Friday 28th January.

Strange things happen when you get to a certain age. Clothes that were once fashionable, begin to look dated and old. Hair sprouts in places where once you had none. And all your friends start to look and behave like your Mum and Dad. Is listening to Radio 2 the future? I'm forty today and I must admit, it does sound old. I open my cards, but refuse to put on the badge my brothers have bought me. My all-time favourite manager, Brian Clough, once remarked in a TV interview, "Whoever said 'life begins at 40' wants shooting. There's not a thing I do now, that I couldn't do better before I was 40."

Sunday 30th January.

Today's the day my Under 9s are playing against arguably the strongest team in the Norman Bairstow League: Wyke. Kind of odd to think of them playing without me being there, but I tell myself I'll phone later to find out the scores.

Paul takes me to a training session with a team called 'Surf,' who he plays for. The sun is up, so sprinting around with the other players is more of a chore than I've been used to lately. Still, I'd swap this for an English winter anytime! The lads are dead friendly and I really enjoy myself. We train for about an hour and a half and finish with a game. Afterwards their manager pulls me to one side wanting to know if I could go with the squad for a tournament in Las Vegas, two weeks from now. I offer up a wry smile and tell him I'm only here for another week, but suggest I'll stay if he pays for my air fare home!

Training over, Paul and I then drive down to Mexico for a couple of days. It's a short trip from San Diego, but seems a million miles from a cold winter in Otley. Whilst my brother and I race dune buggies on the beach in San Bernadino, poor Jimmy is standing frozen between the sticks against Wyke. When I speak to him later he tells me they played very well, but lost 6-2 - Murray scoring twice. The B team only lost 3-2 (Sean scoring both), which is pretty good. Last season they lost 12-0 at Wyke. I remember it well, because there was much derisory laughter from some of their spectators.

Everton got themselves a 2-0 win over Preston North End and will now play Aston Villa in the quarter finals of the F.A. Cup.

51

David Smith

Otley Town Juniors Under 9s
Date of Birth: *8th July 1990*
Position: *Forward*
Nickname: *Quiffy*
Favourite football team: *Leeds Utd*
Favourite food: *Pizza*
Favourite drink: *Fanta*
Best thing outside football:
Playing golf
What I'll be when I'm grown up:
A cricketer

* * * * *

DAVID SMITH
OTLEY TOWN JUNIORS
FORWARD

BRENDAN SUTHERLAND
OTLEY TOWN JUNIORS
GOALKEEPER

Brendan Sutherland

Otley Town Juniors Under 9s
Date of Birth: *15th February 1991*
Position: *Goalkeeper*
Nickname: *Brend*
Favourite football team: *Man. Utd*
Favourite food: *Fish & chips*
Favourite drink: *Lemon & lime*
Best thing outside football:
Playing cricket
What I'll be when I'm grown up:
A sports shopkeeper

* * * * *

FEBRUARY

Tuesday 1st February.

I find it funny, odd, that no one in America seems to walk anywhere. Maybe it's the size of the place and because it takes such a long time getting anywhere. I've always enjoyed getting somewhere under my own steam whenever possible. And given the time, I prefer to walk than call a taxi or catch a bus. Here it's different. Everyone drives everywhere. Also, whereas in England children will sometimes play an impromptu game of football amongst themselves, the American kids seem to need an organised session before they take part in anything. Having said that, equal numbers of boys and girls play soccer in California. In England, there are few girls playing when compared to the millions of boys taking part. A lot of that is history and tradition, which the Americans don't have. But while our women's game is starting to progress back home with the development of the professional league, it has a long way to go to catch up with its equivalent in the States, where the national side are World Champions.

Wedneday 9th February.

I arrive back in England all bleary-eyed, following a long haul from San Diego via Chicago. Can't quite work out what time zone I'm in. It's 8.15am, Manchester time, but the middle of the night in my head.

Later that afternoon, once I've got over the wonderful sight of seeing the kids again, Jimmy fills me in on the goings on at football. The game against Idle Juniors at the weekend had to be cancelled, as the opposition never turned up. Steve Milner and Phil Waite had even gone to the trouble of rolling the pitch, as well as the usual marking out. I must investigate.

Saturday 12th February.

Though it's hard work getting up at 7.30am on a Saturday morning, once I'm in the sports hall at the Aireborough Leisure Centre, I'm almost awake. With me being away, I've forgotten a lot of the boys' names, so it's quite hard to keep order when so-and-so wanders off to the wrong end of the gym and I want so-and-so to come back to the end where everyone else is. Coaching boys of this age is easier in some ways. For one, you don't have to stretch yourself too far as a coach. On the other hand, it can be frustrating when nothing you say seems to make any difference. And that's before they bump their heads in accidental collisons and end up crying. What you do get though, which I love, is plenty of fresh-faced enthusiasm and bags of potential.

In the evening, Ray Rickaby, the Long Lee manager phones to cast some doubt on tomorrow's fixture. It's been raining heavily over the past few days, so I'm not entirely surprised. He'll phone again in the morning.

Sunday 13th February.

The matches are cancelled due to a flooded pitch. I pass on the message to everyone and relax on a Sunday for a change.

Monday 14th February.

First training session back after the holiday. It's great to see everyone again and the evening goes well. Several boys are not available for this weekend's matches, which leaves me a little light on numbers. Adam and Murray are away, whilst Matthew McGlinchey is going to his Mum's wedding. Toby, Matthew Waring and Andrew Jefferies seem to have gone missing. Haven't seen or heard from them for ages. Hope no one else drops out.

Saturday 19th February.

Andrew Kendall and David Smith both cry off. Seriously consider whether to postpone the fixture. I only have eleven boys for two matches. I let Dave Harrison at Gomersal know that I'm struggling to make up two teams, but he understands and says it's OK.

Sunday 20th February.
Away to Gomersal.

We leave for the match, with the Magnificent Eleven. Today, the conditions reign supreme, but the lads play heroically on the slimy pitch. Slipping and sliding, fluid passing is an impossibility, whilst shots stick in goalmouths. The more the boys kick the ball, the more it gathers mud. An endurance test, orange and black stripes turn grey in the battle. The spectators shout encouragement more in hope than anything. Then suddenly, Josh and James combine, whipping the ball to Michael, whose first time right foot shot flashes into the net. 1-0 to Otley. Josh then gets hacked down by a **desperate Gomersal defence**, as he attempts to dribble through the swamp. Unbelievably, no penalty! In the second half, tackles fly, chances are missed and a hand-ball goes unpunished, before Josh exacts revenge by slipping past three defenders and cracking home the second goal.

Jack and Jimmy change places for the B team game, with 'Five' taking the gloves, whilst Michael and James share another half each. The result, though a bit of a travesty in terms of possession, is reversed and Gomersal win this encounter 2-0.

The Magnificent Eleven ride away with their mums and dads, filthy dirty, but undaunted and full of spirit. Today wasn't a day for faint hearts. Winning and losing came second to 'just taking part.' I wonder what those kids in California would have made of it.

Later that afternoon Joe and I watch Everton play Aston Villa in the F.A. Cup quarter-final. As it's on Sky TV, we watch it at the Yew Tree pub in Otley. Everton lose 2-1, so I'm disappointed. I was hoping to take Joe and Jimmy to Wembley.

Monday 21st February.

I'm feeling a little downhearted this morning, in light of Everton's demise yesterday. No training today, as it's half-term, but I've already made arrangements for games at Shipley next Sunday.

Sunday 27th February.
Away to Shipley.

Last weekend was a picture postcard next to this. Wild, wet and windy does not do it justice. It's also the kind of game to make my hair turn grey, or fall out altogether. We're kicking up the slope in the first half, against the strong wind and I play Josh at the back with Max in the first half, just to counter the elements. It's all going quite well, until Jimmy miscues a goal-kick. The ball goes straight to one of their forwards, who volleys back over Jimmy's head and into the net.

At the break, with the rain lashing down, I rally the lads, confident we can get something out of the game. In the second half, the two sides go at each other hammer and tongs. End to end football at its best. Josh pushes up into midfield and he's brilliant. Max and Jack aren't too far behind him, but still we can't score. At this stage I'm kicking and heading everything for them. Michael and Matthew M. go close, whilst Jimmy makes amends for his first half error with a brilliant two handed diving save. My stomach's in knots and time is running out. With only six or seven minutes left, Josh goes on another dribble, squares the ball to Murray and he fires home. I immediately throw my arms and the sweatshirt I'm holding into the air in triumph. The boys have all got grins on their faces, but they're not finished. With barely two minutes remaining, Michael swings over a corner and somehow it evades everyone and ends up in the net. It's Shipley's first defeat of the season and probably our best win to date. I'm delighted. It's always nice to win games, but to beat good sides and play well in terrible conditions, makes the achievement all the sweeter.

I shake hands with Phil Ainge, the Shipley manager. We both know we've witnessed one hell of a game and that all the boys from both sides deserve credit.

Whilst the A team put up a fantastic performance in their match, the B team fair less well, losing 4-0. This despite more than matching Shipley in the first half. At 0-0, I felt we had a chance, but three quick goals after half-time destroyed the fight and spirit of the boys and a late goal towards the end sealed our fate.

Nevertheless and despite being totally drenched, I head for home with some satisfaction, until I hear that Joe's Under 12s have lost their cup semi-final at Harrogate Railway. I wish I'd been able to watch him play.

Monday 28th February.

I really don't understand the phenomena of Pokemon cards, but kids seem to be in a frenzy over them. Articles in the national papers report millions of pounds worth of sales, with children buying and swapping these fantasy monster items at a rate of knots. Some papers even report kids being attacked and robbed of their collections. What's going on? Nobody ever tried to take my 1970 England World Cup Esso coin collection away from me. And who or what are Bulbasaur and Tangela anyway? Tonight I get tough and tell Matthew M and his crew to save the oggling of cards until after the training session has finished.

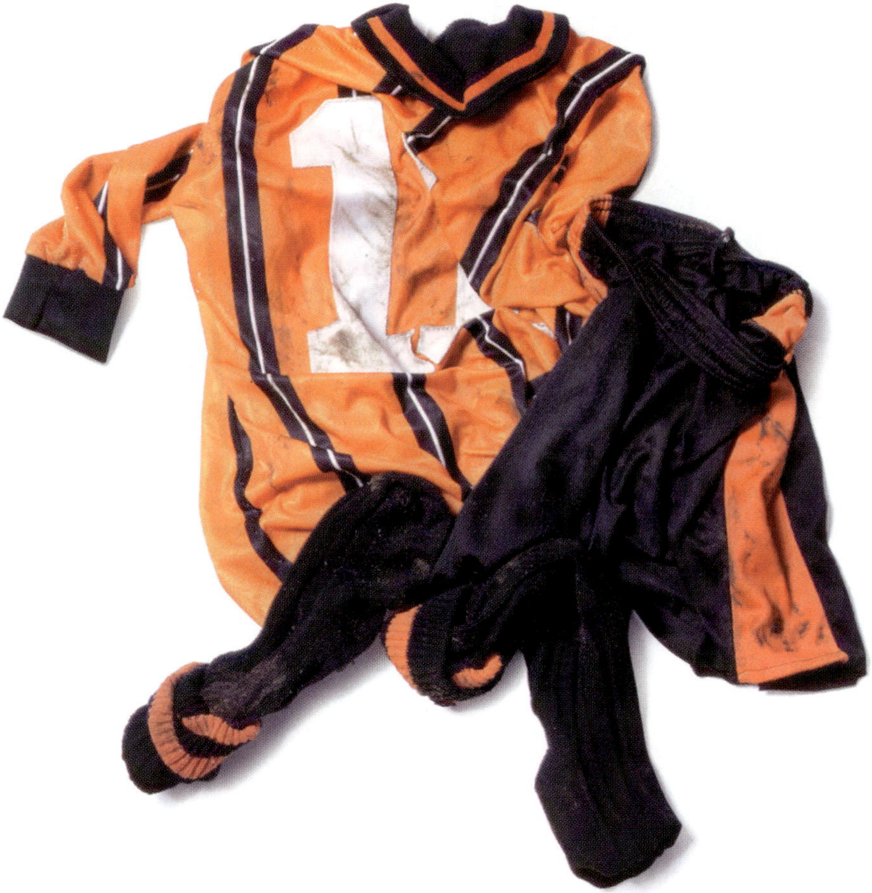

MATTHEW WARING
OTLEY TOWN JUNIORS — MIDFIELD

Matthew Waring

Otley Town Juniors Under 9s
Date of Birth: *19th March 1991*
Position: *Midfield or defender*
Nickname: *Tish*
Favourite football team: *Leeds Utd*
Favourite food: *Pizza*
Favourite drink: *Coke*
Best thing outside football:
Riding my bike
What I'll be when I'm grown up:
A footballer

* * * * *

James Dalby

Otley Town Juniors Under 9s
Date of Birth: *7th July 1991*
Position: *Forward or midfield*
Nickname: *None*
Favourite football team: *Leeds Utd*
Favourite food: *Mashed potato*
Favourite drink: *Pepsi*
Best thing outside football:
Playing on my Game Boy
What I'll be when I'm grown up:
A footballer

* * * * *

JAMES DALBY
OTLEY TOWN JUNIORS — FORWARD

MARCH

Saturday 4th March.

At nine o'clock, I'm coaching the Striker Awards at Aireborough. In the afternoon, I play for Otley Town Reserves in the Harrogate League Cup semi-final at Ilkley. We win 2-0, so I'll be playing in my first cup final since I can't remember when.

Sunday 5th March.
Home to Idle Juniors.

Up at 7.30am. An hour later Jimmy and I are at the club, where the ground is slightly hard following an overnight frost. I open up the garage where we keep the goals, nets, etc. and discover there is no line marker. I assume someone has taken it up to Wharfemeadow Fields where the older lads play. After a lot of waiting around, I try to phone Ron Brown, who runs the Under 11s and when I eventually get hold of him, he's passed the marker on to one of the other managers. I curse and despair in frustration. By 9.15am, I've had enough waiting, so I set off for Wharfemeadows. Half-way there, the line marker passes me in the back of the Under 16s manager's car. By now it's a black comedy, with everyone having a laugh at my expense. So Starsky and Hutch style, I spin my car round and tear back to the club.

By 10.00am, I've calmed down a bit. The pitch is marked out and the nets are up. My players are all here, but there's no opposition. I phone Wayne Potter, the Idle manager, but his wife answers telling me he's set off already.

At 10.20am, they arrive with only eight or nine players to play two matches. They also have a couple of girls on their team, which completely foxes some of my lads. When the games start, you can see them not sure about tackling them. In spite of that the A team are too strong for the visitors and at half-time, we're 3-0 up and cruising. Michael's got two of the goals, one direct from a corner for the second week running and Matthew M's got the other.

In the second period it very nearly goes horribly wrong. Thinking we've won it already, we ease off the gas, whilst Idle start to compete. Had it not been for Jack Wood, we might even have lost. He at least has the common sense to try and hold the defence together. At 3-2, I'm losing my cool a bit, trying to gee them up. Even Max is having an off day, which is almost unheard of. Only a late and deciding goal from Matthew M gets us out of gaol. At the end, I gather in the boys for a post match chat. Normally I'd be congratulating them, or pointing out in a constructive way, a feature they could improve on. Today I'm cross. Against a side we should have beaten comfortably, the boys stopped trying. Still, they're only young, so hopefully it's a lesson learned.

Simon Wood kindly agreed to referee the first match, even though I know he prefers to just watch. Unfortunately, with Steve Milner working and in the absence of anyone else suitable, I have to ref the second

60

game. This is something I hate doing because I can't be anything other than impartial. I can't shout instructions and I can't observe what's happening to my team properly. I still think like a coach as I'm running around, whistle in hand, but sometimes I've become so distracted wishing Adam would cover round for Callum, or Lloyd would just pass it simple to Sean instead of dribbling all the time, that I forget a referee needs to concentrate too. "Whose throw is it ref?" Errm....

The B team lose after leading through James Dalby's goal. They're a little unlucky and do at least try harder than the A team did. In the end, with the scores level at one-all, James Dalby handles the ball in his own area, protecting his face from a shot. I have to give a penalty. The tall girl on their team puts it away and Idle win 2-1. Judging by their reactions at the end, it must be their first win of the season, so despite my own and the boys' disappointment, I can understand their joy. That was very much us last season.

Monday 6th March.

After training tonight, there's a meeting at the club. The agenda includes the visit on Easter Saturday of the Hessle Juniors Club, from Hull. It's their annual trip and after playing against our juniors in the morning, they're all going to watch Huddersfield Town versus Bolton Wanderers in the afternoon. From our club's point of view, there's a lot to be gained from their visit, not least financially. Of course there's a lot of organising to do. With building work going on at the club, bricks and breeze blocks abound. New changing rooms and showers are planned with next season in mind. There's now a new roof in place, which hopefully means the rain will stay outside on wet weekends. Interior decoration is in need of help, as well as the more pressing requirements to satisfy an impending health and safety check. Without these improvements, the club would undoubtedly be forced to close. We all agree to help tidy up the club before Easter Saturday. There's also the question of whether to lay on a marquee for the Hessle club, as well as ordering extra beer, soft drinks and food for a barbeque. I volunteer to organise skips for the tidy-up and to mark out pitches on Good Friday.

Aside from that business and with the future of the club in mind, I suggest holding a football morning at the club to generate Under 7s and 8s age groups for next season. I am prepared to run a coaching session as an introduction to Otley Town and will probably ask Martin Ibbetson, the first team manager at the club, to help me out on the day.

Friday 10th March.

I finally remember to phone Julie Brotherton about hiring two skips for next Saturday morning.

Sunday 12th March.
Away to Long Lee.

The Big One. Top of the league versus us in third. A chance to avenge our 5-0 defeat in September. We are a stronger, better team now. A shame Matthew Waring won't be playing. With him and Josh in the side, I'd even fancy us to win. But no matter. We'd beaten second placed Shipley, why not Long Lee?

I agonised over the team, even though it almost picked itself and finally decided to play Adam in the A team for the first time, in defence with Max. This would leave the B team short, but it would be worth it for this one. I told the boys it was their toughest game yet. The Big One. Get ready, be quick, be strong, be confident. Enjoy yourselves, pass the ball and move.

We warmed up. We were ready. We were 2-0 down before we woke up. Long Lee were faster and stronger than us. For fifteen minutes we hardly got out of our own penalty area.

At half-time, I rallied the troops. It was not beyond us, we're as good as

61

them. Just think quicker, pass the ball quicker, try harder. We can do it. And for the whole of the second half, we played with the fire, passion and skill that I know we're capable of. It was end to end. Max was outstanding, as was Josh. Jack was his usual intelligent self, whilst up front Michael and Matthew M kept the home defence busy. Long Lee had their chances - Jimmy made a good save, Adam even headed against his own bar - then Josh scored. A great goal from distance. We were back in it. The home supporters were more anxious, I could sense it. I hoped we'd score another. I kicked and headed every ball for them. But in the end, it wasn't quite enough and we lose 2-1. The lads were disappointed, but I was proud of them and told them so. Winning would have been great, but to play the way we did gave me the most satisfaction. I felt great. Even the B team's 9-0 drubbing didn't diminish the achievement today.

Monday 13th March.

For once, I haven't really got a plan as I arrive at the gym tonight, but considering the B team's weak performance yesterday, I concentrate on passing. Short and quick, watching closely for correct technique. We then have a short spell on heading, before finishing with small-sided games, where I encourage the boys to talk to each other, giving free-kicks for no communication at all.

Tuesday 14th March.

Bev Hall phones regarding Toby's disappearance since Christmas. They're moving house, so things have been fraught. But Toby still wants to play, though training might be a problem. I tell Bev to get her son down to the club this weekend for the B team match against Oakworth.

Wednesday 15th March.

I attend a coaching demonstration at Armley Sports Centre, put on by Jon Conway and John Hall of the Leeds Coaches Association. It features the structure and practices that make up the Striker Awards which I'm involved in on Saturday mornings. A useful evening to watch and take special note of the skills required to make the higher standards of achievement within the scheme. There are about thirty other coaches present. Of course, it's all fuel to throw at my boys, but I often wonder about 'over-coaching' them. Take Matthew McGlinchey for example, who's a wonderfully talented dribbler. Maybe the best I have. He's also top scorer and yet I hear myself asking him to pass the ball. To dribble here and not dribble there. I want the boys to think for themselves, so maybe sometimes I should shut up. The great Ferenc Puskas once commented, *"I am grateful to my father for all the coaching he did not give me."*

Saturday 18th March.

Just when I thought everything was going swimmingly, I get injured playing for Otley Reserves. 1-0 down in a local derby, I come off worst in a fifty-fifty tackle and have to limp off. I know straightaway it's not any old bruise either. I can barely walk back to the changing room and I'm last out of the showers and into the bar. Somehow I manage to drive home and when I get there, I stick an ice-pack on my leg and start feeling sorry for myself. I just hope my season isn't over, especially with the Cup Final to come.

Sunday 19th March.
Home to Silsden and Oakworth.

Sleeping was a problem last night. Every time I moved, it felt like my leg was on fire. Finding a comfortable position was impossible and so moving this morning is agony. It takes me about twenty minutes to get downstairs. Jimmy looks on helplessly as I embark on the momentous task of slipping into my tracksuit bottoms. I stare at my trainers, trying to figure a way of avoiding the hellish inferno of putting them on. Thereafter, each subsequent task becomes a massive feat of achievement. It takes all of my willpower to hobble to the car. Fortunately, the gear is already packed in the boot, so that's one less job.

At the club, I move in slow-motion on to the playing area, markers at the ready. But before I've got very far, my pathetic efforts are rescued by Steve Milner, who gets out the line marker. Rod Almond gives him a hand to put up the goals and nets, whilst I totter about like a lemon.

Though I can still manage a pre-match pep talk, Phil Waite has to warm the boys up before the matches. I even have a bench to sit on today, though that becomes redundant once the first game begins. Pain or no pain, I can't relax and sit still. Shouting instructions and encouragement somehow feels more natural when stood up.

By half-time we're 2-0 up against Silsden and playing well. Jack and Josh are the scorers. By the end, we've missed a hatfull of chances, but still win 4-0. Michael and Josh again, the second half scorers.

In the second match, I give little Andrew Kendall the goalkeeping gloves. He's asked me a few times for an opportunity, so in spite of his size, I take a chance. He doesn't disappoint, fearlessly throwing himself about. If he'd been a foot taller, he'd have got the high ball that flew over his head for the opening goal. The B team eventually draw 1-1 with Oakworth, with Murray Simm getting the goal.

When the football is over, most of the rest of the day is spent with my leg under an ice-pack.

Monday 20th March.

Still can't walk without pain. The constant icing of my leg hasn't brought out any bruising. Coaching is difficult tonight. Whilst my mouth does the talking, I use Joe as my legs to demonstrate the art of shielding the ball. It's something we've done as a group before, so it's not as if I'm asking them to grasp a totally new technique.

Saturday 25th March.

Phil Waite phones to tell me about Josh's invitation to play for Barnsley. Josh wants to play for their Under 9s, but doesn't want to let us down. I tell

63

him not to worry, we'll win without him. I wish him well and hope he enjoys the experience. To be honest, it wouldn't surprise me if he makes the grade. I know it's much too early to say for sure, but the lad has got talent and I haven't seen anyone better in our league this season. He also seems very level headed and without the arrogance that you might expect from someone of that ability.

Sunday 26th March.
Away to Bingley.

Everyone's clocks go forward, except mine. At 8.00am (my time), Simon Wood calls (9.00am everyone else's time) to let me know that they're all waiting for me down the club. Jimmy is still in his pyjamas and neither of us have had our breakfast, but within minutes we're off in the car, trying to wake up and shake off the embarrassment.

It's a lovely sunny morning and despite my doziness, we still get to Bingley in good time. Toby however is late meeting us at the pitch, so I have a few worrying minutes wondering whether or not we've enough players.

With Josh unavailable, there are no subs, which means Jimmy in goal, even though he'll play in midfield for the B team. Toby plays in defence with Max. He does OK, though I'm constantly having to talk to him, telling him where to position himself. We go a goal down, despite being the better team. Then, just before half-time, Lloyd breaks away from outside his own area and passes to Matthew M, who scores the equaliser.

In the second half, Matthew M, who's had a fantastic game, puts us in front and we look like winning.

Then out of nothing it happens. The Goal of the Season. Our equivalent of the goal John Barnes scored for England against Brazil. Jack Wood, (remember his name), pulls the ball out of the sky, evading a crowd of

64

Bingley shirts. He beats one man. He beats another. And another. He crosses the half-way line, a trail of floundering defenders behind him. I'm now willing him to score. Everyone is. The tension mounts. He beats the last defender. He shoots. He scores. It's one hell of a goal. And he knows it. His arms are aloft and for a moment he's David Beckham. It takes me all afternoon to stop smiling.

So we win 3-1 and it's followed by another cracking match. The B team play superbly, but somehow can't score. It's end to end, before Bingley take the lead on half-time. Chance after chance goes begging in the second period, until Sean comes to the rescue with an equaliser. After so many recent defeats they deserve a bit of luck, which is what they need to score again. Unfortunately they don't get it. Right at the end, Bingley grab a winner and we lose 2-1.

Monday 27th March.

I often bang on about technique and improving it. With some boys it is there naturally. Personally, I always had to work at mine.

One Sunday morning back in the early 1970s, I was playing for my local junior side, but having little success getting past the defender who was marking me. At half-time, my manager pulled me to one side. "Mark. You've got the speed to beat that lad, but you're not thinking about the best way to do it. If you keep the ball closer to your feet when you're taking him on, you'll stand a better chance."

The thing I learned from that was to use my brain. And even though I never realised a good dribbling technique for myself, I compensated by learning to pass and move off the ball.

If I have a single aim for all of my boys, it is for them to develop the ability to think for themselves. To have that is to have self-belief and confidence. And that will reap rewards on the pitch.

In 'My Life and the Beautiful Game' (1977), Pele remarked, *"I go much faster than those who run without thinking."*

Michael Beecroft

Otley Town Juniors Under 9s
Date of Birth: 25th August 1990
Position: Forward
Nickname: Waspy
Favourite football team: Leeds Utd
Favourite food: Sausages
Favourite drink: Coke
Best thing outside football:
Playing with friends
What I'll be when I'm grown up:
A footballer

* * * * *

MICHAEL BEECROFT
OTLEY TOWN JUNIORS — FORWARD

SEAN BROTHERTON
OTLEY TOWN JUNIORS — FORWARD

Sean Brotherton

Otley Town Juniors Under 9s
Date of Birth: 23rd April 1991
Position: Forward
Nickname: The Prawn
Favourite football team: Leeds Utd
Favourite food: Fish & chips
Favourite drink: Orange
Best thing outside football:
Driving tractors
What I'll be when I'm grown up:
A footballer

* * * * *

APRIL

Saturday 1st April.

Only when I'm not playing football do I realise how much it still means to me. The frustration of my latest injury and the thought it may keep me from competing in the Harrogate League Cup Final on Easter Monday, more than puts a dampener on my weekend. Watching is just torture. When I play I feel alive. It gives me more pleasure than almost anything. I've just got to be part of the action. Today, watching the reserves at Otley, I try to be supportive and shout encouragement from the dug-out, but deep down I'm miserable and I hate it.

Sunday 2nd April.
Away to Cullingworth.

Mother's Day. And what better way for my mum to spend a morning than standing in the rain watching her grandson play football. She must enjoy it or presumably she wouldn't bother.

Mum always claimed that she spent her entire time as a mother with the washing machine on cleaning dirty kit. Even on Christmas Day, when we'd be out playing football of some kind. And although she often said she hated the game, I can still remember the times she'd watch me play - somehow always appearing more conspicuous than anyone else, with her bright red coat and knee-length white boots. Although that was embarrassing, deep down I was glad she was there.

Only one fixture today, as the A team will be playing on Wednesday evening against Idle Saints. When we get to Cullingworth, we have the luxury of a changing room - which is handy with the rain setting in. Mum waits in the car whilst I name the team and keep them inside out of the wet. Murray and Matthew M are playing for the B team today, as they can't make it on Wednesday. Jack's also with us, so we should do well. When we run out onto the pitch, we're quickly followed by a rather 'official looking' referee, dressed in the traditional black. Most of the time, it's all very informal, with someone's dad doing-the-do wearing a pair of old pumps and some jogging bottoms. This guy looks like he means business and at first I'm impressed. When the game's in progress however, I notice him taking a rather tough line. And when, in the second half, he gives a foul throw against us, I go mad, watching him give the ball to the home side. "Why don't you just let my lad take it again?" I shout despairingly. "That's how he learns to do it properly!" It's the wrong thing to say. Contrary to my own perceptions, in the referee's mind it's a World Cup Final and any decision contested is a highly serious matter. He sprints over and gives me a good dressing down, much to the amusement of my players and I have to bite my lip. Even after the game, when I go up to him, smilingly to offer an olive branch, he barks, "You stick to coaching and leave the refereeing to me!" What a jerk. Still, despite him the boys play very well and win 2-1. Birthday boys, Murray and Jack score the goals. And even my mum agrees with me on the referee.

Monday 3rd April.

I am the running, running, running man. I run and run as fast as I can. I love to run. To be out in the fresh air. It gives me energy for life. It gives me energy for coaching. Tonight I need the energy. They are a lively bunch sometimes. It helps that my injury has improved sufficiently for me to run about a bit. Thankfully, this should be the last training session inside at Prince Henry's gym. Next week we'll be outside.

Back home, I speak to Malcolm Dobinson about the dates for the Otley 6-a-side Tournament next month. When I realise he's planning it for the weekend of the F.A. Cup Final, I quizz him. "Malcolm, you do realise the tournament will clash with the F.A. Cup Final don't you?" (Malcolm): "It be right." (Me): What do you mean, it be right?" (Malcolm, after a pause): " It be right."

Wednesday 5th April.
Home to Idle Saints.

This should really be an away match, but Idle have had trouble with their pitch and wanted to come to us. Tonight it's a bit of a rush getting to the club on time, as I'm working until quarter to six. When I arrive, some of the boys and parents are already there waiting. I quickly mark out a pitch and get things ready. I tell my lads it's an evening kick-off because the Sky TV cameras are going to be here, but I don't think they believe me. With or without Andy Gray and crew, we win easily 4-0 - James, an own goal and Michael (2), the scorers - but it leaves me a little unsatisfied. (I'm getting fussy.) Jack tells his brother Barney that we're "grinding out results without playing well." A future TV pundit in the making.

Sunday 9th April.
Home to Shelf and Wilsden.

David Smith won't play today, because his brother Stuart has worn his boots without asking. He will only set foot on the field when he has a new pair. As David is my very own Stan Collymore - his dad's own description, not mine - it comes as no great surprise, but this close to kick-off, David has no chance of getting his way. He tends to pick and choose his games at the best of times - often around the weather - but this is a new excuse.

The rest of the lads soldier on without him and produce a really marvellous morning's entertainment. The A team win 2-0, Murray and Jack scoring again, whilst the B team win 5-2 - their best performance of the season - Lloyd, James, Matthew Waring and Matthew McGlinchey (2) scoring. And because it might be my last opportunity to give everyone (bar David Smith) a game, there's a C team match against Wilsden B. Sean scores twice in a 3-3 draw, with an equaliser from James in the very last minute.

Monday 10th April.

Michael makes a tackle. It's only in training admittedly, but that's progress. A boy with lots of ability - quick and with a rocket of a shot on him, he's also a lad who tends to be rather shy of the physical side of football. Until tonight it seems. Back in his own area, winning the ball with a challenge Matthew Waring and Max make every week. If that's what he's going to do in matches, Michael will be a really tremendous player.

Tonight, it's all very upbeat, on a lovely sunny evening outside at Otley Town F.C. The boys love the relays - fetching and dribbling balls, as it's fun as well as being competitive.

Afterwards, I coach the boys on a

69

keep ball exercise, which the A team lads in particular, cope well with. Those with lesser technique struggle to string more than a couple of passes together.

But though it probably passes unnoticed by many, Michael's brilliant interception makes my evening. A small, but significant development.

Tuesday 11th April.

My moment of truth. After missing several games since my injury, I'm desperate to get back into the action in time for the Cup Final in a fortnight. I'm playing in an evening fixture for Otley Town Reserves, down at the Club. For forty minutes it goes like a dream. I'm playing great, we're winning 3-0 and my leg feels fine. Just before half-time, I'm the victim of two late tackles and my leg is on fire again. My season, including the chance to lift the cup, is over. Words cannot express how I feel.

Wednesday 12th April.

Seeing my children play any sport is usually a real pleasure for me. Tonight, watching Joe play football for the Under 12s is very definitely not fun. My blasted leg is hell, it's cold and it's raining heavily. Bad enough for me, but how Joe or the rest of the team get through the match in those conditions, I don't know. They all deserve a medal.

Thursday 13th April.

Today, I should have been travelling with the Leeds Coaches Association, on their trip to Derby County. Unfortunately, due to heavy work commitments, I can't go. It's a big disappointment, but as I'm still in a lot of pain with my right leg, getting about is tricky.

The last two years, I've been on similar trips with the Association, to Newcastle and Coventry, which were great. At Newcastle, we observed a day's coaching with the Youth team. Last season at Coventry, it was an opportunity to watch Gordon Strachan oversee a morning with their first team squad. (Coming off the back of a win over Everton the day before, I had kept my mouth shut when talk of boxing off Duncan Ferguson and other such tactics were mentioned.)

All in all these trips are great to attend and certainly fill me with lots of ideas to incorporate in my own coaching sessions.

Saturday 15th April.

My leg is still sore, so I can't run about at all, never mind kick a ball. I also feel a bit flat, so the coaching at Aireborough doesn't go as well as normal. Still, with Easter almost upon us, I'm due a couple of weeks off on a Saturday morning. I feel like I need a break. Today, some of the boys mess about so much, I have to call them in for a stern word. "You're here to enjoy yourselves, but if you want to learn something you must listen when I'm talking otherwise we won't get anything done. If you want to muck about then go join a crèche." To which, one little boy replies, "What's a creche?"

Sunday 16th April.

No matches. We should've been competing in the Norman Bairstow 5-a-side Tournament, but the event has been cancelled this year. Instead and as a bit of end of season fun, I take all the boys and one or two hardy parents to the Richard Dunn Sports Centre in Bradford. The attraction is the Jungle Pool and in particular the two water slides. Some of the lads either can't or don't fancy coming, so there's about fourteen children in all, including Maisie and a couple of other girls. One and a half hours later, I'm worn out, even if the kids aren't.

Monday 17th April.

Barnsley have signed up Josh to play for their Academy, which means he'll not be part of my team plans for next season. I'm disappointed for the team's sake, though pleased at the same time for Josh.

Friday 21st April.

Good Friday and Suj is up for the weekend again. Within an hour or so of arriving off a train at Guiseley, I've got him down to Otley Town helping me mark out pitches for the Hessle visit tomorrow. It's a nightmare, dodging the heavy downpours of rain, whilst trying to get joy from the godforsaken line marker.

By 4.30pm, there's still loads to do, but we've got a match to see. Tonight, it's the Merseyside derby at Goodison Park and Suj has got tickets. And a decent game it turns out to be, despite a blank scoreline. Both sides play good, passing football and even though I'm biased, we are robbed! Right at the end of the game, deep into injury time, Liverpool's keeper, Westerveld, takes a free-kick from his own area. The ball cannons off the back of the retreating Don Hutchison and into the net. The crowd goes mad. But Graham Poll, the referee, however, bottles the decision, disallows the goal and walks off the pitch for the end of the match, surrounded by angry protesting Everton players. At midnight in a bar in Knotty Ash, Suj and I are still up in arms.

Saturday 22nd April.
Home to Hessle.

Despite not getting to bed until 1.30am, I'm up at seven o'clock and down the club by twenty past. Ron Brown and several others are there already. It's raining, so putting up the nets and marking out pitches is really fun. Fortunately, we've a new line marker that actually works, so the job gets done quicker. Just before 9.00am, I nip home for some breakfast and bring Joe and Jimmy back with me.

The Under 9s aren't playing until 11.20am, so it's an opportunity for me to watch Joe. Unfortunately, the coaches from Hessle are late arriving, so there's a little bit of nervous shuffling of feet beforehand wondering if they'll turn up. When they do it's a rush to get all the matches on, as Hessle have to be away by one o'clock, to go to the Huddersfield v. Bolton game. The place is absolutely packed and luckily the rain seems to have stopped.

I watch a good part of Joe's match, before nipping off to pick up Matthew Waring from the Lawnswood Arms. Normally his dad, Shane brings him, but he's working today, so I offered to help.

The Under 9s matches kick off more or less on time, though we're only playing fifteen minutes each way, instead of the normal twenty. The game is initially close, until Matthew W scores a cracker from distance. After that, the A team win easily. Matthew M gets two, as does Jack. Josh and Sean get the others in a 7-0 victory. The B team also win, 7-1. Murray scores the opening goal, though the best bit for me is seeing Jimmy score his first goal of the season. His face is a picture as the ball hits the net - somewhere between excitement and surprise. (Pretty much how I react when I score these days.) James, Lloyd and Sean with a hat-trick get the others. By the end, I'm happy, though I've also had enough. When the nets are all taken down and put away, I'm more than ready for a nice cup of tea and a sit down.

Monday 24th April.

Otley Town Reserves versus Harrogate Railway Reserves in the Harrogate Premier League Cup Final.

It's an odd experience. All the players are excited, naturally enough, but I feel somewhat detached. When we get to Boroughbridge, we walk about a lot, because we're really early. Dave Crombleholme, the manager and one or two of the older players seem to understand my disappointment and try to keep me involved. I help by filling water bottles and buckets, before doing the pre-match warm-up.

When we kick-off I watch from the dug-out hoping they win and shouting encouragement. But inside it hurts not being involved. When they do win, after extra-time, I'm dead chuffed for the team, but feel numb watching them pick up the cup without me.

Wednesday 26th April.
I try to arrange a couple of friendly matches for the Under 9s. No one I call is in, apart from Darren Gregory at Cowling. He's interested and will call back tomorrow.

Sunday 30th April.
I'm turning into Rip Van Winkle. With no football to get up for yesterday and today, I've slept until nearly nine o'clock.

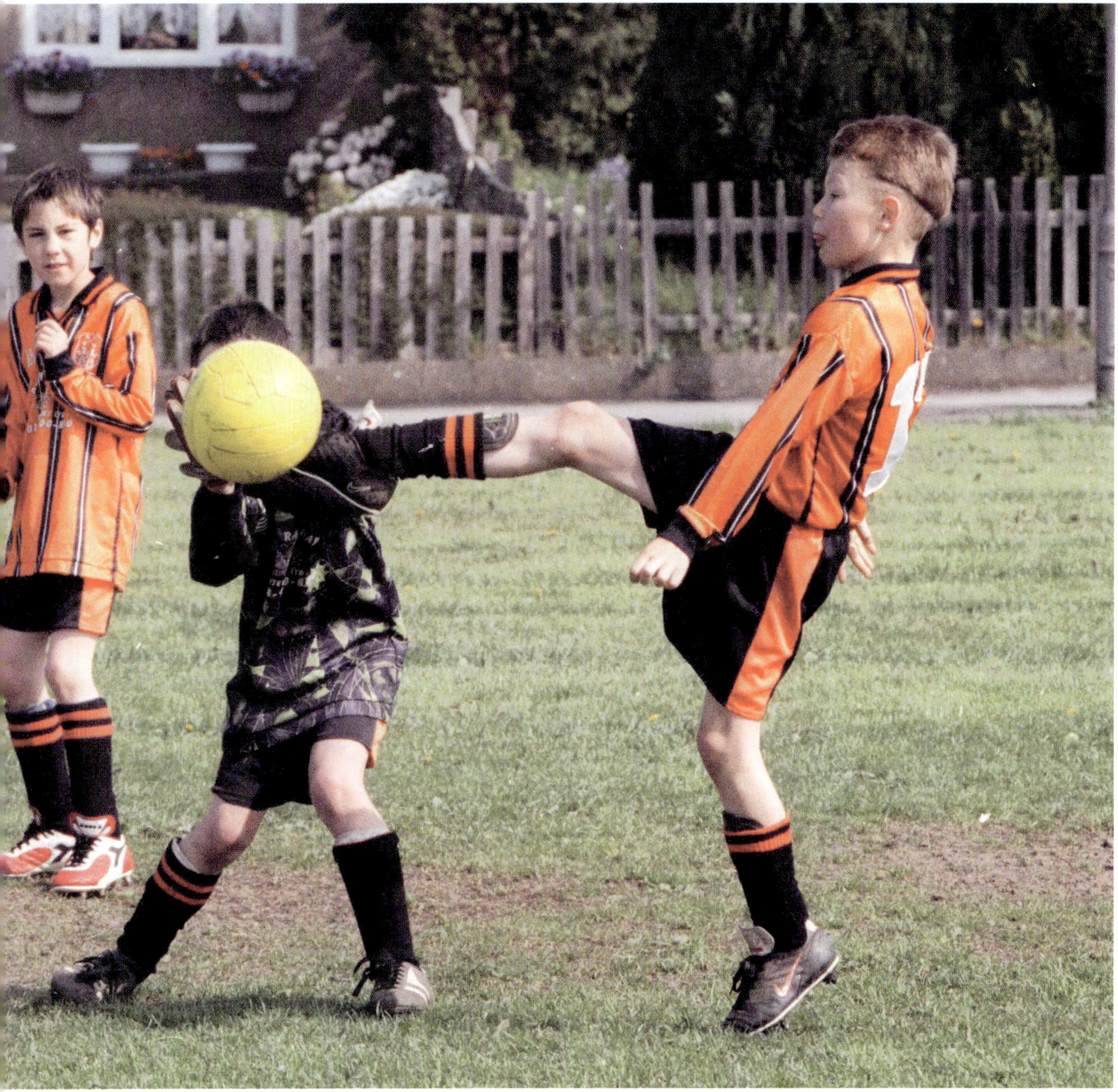

MARK CURRIE
OTLEY TOWN JUNIORS
COACH

Mark Currie

Otley Town Juniors Under 9s
Date of Birth: *28th January 1960*
Position: *Coach*
Nickname: *None*
Favourite football team: *Everton*
Favourite food: *Raspberry Pavlova*
Favourite drink: *Guinness*
Best thing outside football:
Using my imagination
What I'll be when I'm grown up:
A veteran footballer

* * * * *

MAY

Monday 2nd May.

I upset Julie because I've organised a training session on a Bank Holiday. She thinks I'm completely obsessed and totally blanks me thereafter. To be honest, I hadn't realised it was a holiday until just before the weekend. By then, having sent out letters to parents, I couldn't be bothered with the hassle of phoning round everyone to cancel. Still, in hindsight, it's a mistake. Only eight boys turn up, probably proving Julie right that people have better things to do on a Bank Holiday than ferry their son to football.

Tuesday 3rd May.

Phone all the parents whose sons weren't at training yesterday about Sunday's matches. We're meeting at 10.00am for a 10.30am kick-off at the club. Mark Hardcastle from Weston Lane then calls regarding a friendly match on the 14th. He also reminds me that the Wharfedale League are using Otley Town for their 6-a-side tournament on Sunday, which kind of scuppers my plans. After cursing myself for forgetting about their tournament, I phone Chris Lawson at Weston Lane, who's organising the thing. He says we can play our matches against Cowling on their pitch, seeing as they're using ours. Great stuff. So now all I have to do is phone all my parents again and rearrange everything......

At 8.00pm, there's a meeting at the club to discuss the arrangements for the Wharfedale Tournament (ha, ha!) plus the latest developments regarding the improvements to the clubhouse, showers, etc.

Wednesday 4th May.

Shane Waring phones to tell me he can't bring his son Matthew to football on Sunday, so I agree to pick Matthew up from his mum, Helen at the Lawnswood Arms again.

Friday 6th May.

I phone John Hutchinson, who's coming down on Sunday to take some photos of the boys, including a team picture. I also call all the parents to ensure everyone meets at the same time.

Saturday 7th May.

Pop down to the club with Joe and spend a couple of hours assembling Coca-Cola goals in preparation for the Wharfedale Tournament tomorrow. Chris Lawson has already marked out a pitch for me at Weston Lane and when I see him he gives me the keys to their clubhouse.

Sunday 7th May.
Home to Cowling.

Wake up at 4.00am to the wailing of a tomcat and can't get back to sleep again. When I do get out of bed at 7.45am, I feel knackered. At 8.45am, Janet Milner calls to tell me Max has been ill in the night and isn't up to playing. "That's a shame," I say, "but if he's well enough, at least get him there for the team photograph. It wouldn't be right to have a picture without him."

At just after 9.00am, I set off with Jimmy and Joe (who's coming to watch his brother), to pick up Matthew Waring. He's there nice and early, so we're back in Otley and at Weston Lane by 9.35am. John has just arrived with his little son Alex in tow. He sets up his camera on a tripod by the side of the pitch, just in time to see Matthew W knock it over with a football. No damage done, John snaps away as each of the lads arrive.

I open up the clubhouse and drag out the nets with the help of Rod Almond. Max turns up with his mum, looking a bit washed out, but I'm pleased he's here. John takes the team photograph just as cars from Cowling arrive. (Bet someone is pulling a funny face and spoiling it.)

Cowling tear into us at the start of the A team match and for ten minutes, barely give us a kick. It's a hot sunny day, so eventually the pace drops, which suits us more. By then I'm already missing Max, who can only watch as Cowling score from a long punt forward. The ball comes off the back of Matthew W's head and with Jimmy rooted to his line, it lands at the feet of a Cowling forward and flies high into the net. By half-time though, Matthew M has scored a couple of beauties and we're back in it, 2-1 up and playing well. At the break, Max persuades me he's alright to play, so I give him a game in place of Toby. Within a few minutes, he's not right, so Janet takes him home and packs him off to bed. Meantime, Josh adds a third goal for us and the game looks won. Matthew W then gets blistered heels, has to come off and against the run of play, Cowling score again. For a moment I'm a bit nervous, though incredibly we catch fire and score four times in the last five minutes. The pick of them, a flashing drive from Michael Beecroft which fairly tears into the net. (I can almost feel all the spectators around me take a sharp intake of breath.) Matthew M gets another two goals, so we win 7-2, which is really tough on Cowling.

The B team don't do quite as well, though at one stage they're winning 2-0. Once James and David have put us in the driving seat, I fully expect us to win easily. Cowling though, with several younger boys in their team, fight back and deserve their eventual 3-2 victory. In a funny way, I'm pleased for Darren Gregory, the Cowling manager, who I don't think expected his B team to do as well as they did.

It's getting on for 1.00pm once I've packed everything away and dropped Matthew W off at Otley Town, where Helen has come to pick him up. I grab a drink and a burger with my sons, whilst watching a little of the football in the Wharfedale Tournament, before heading home. The rest of the day is football-free.

Monday 9th May.

The sun is still out, which makes coaching a real pleasure. Why can't junior football be a summer sport? Tonight, there are fifteen boys, plus a new lad called George. I incorporate the relay drill again, which goes down well, plus a lot of shooting practice. This allows me to give some attention to the goalkeepers, Jimmy and Simon Harris, who was surprisingly good in goal for the B team yesterday.

When I give out the teamsheets for our final matches of the season on Sunday, I also give out slips for the boys to vote for their player of the season. I hear someone mutter he might vote for himself.

Everton's penultimate match of the season against Leeds at Elland Road, ends in a 1-1 draw, which takes the Blues up to 10th in the league.

Wednesday 10th May.

Chris Stewart phones to say he's got me two tickets for the England v Brazil match at Wembley on May 29th. This is great news for Joe, but only two tickets means I can't take Jimmy as well.

Saturday 13th May.

I've still got a problem with my right leg, which causes some discomfort during my morning session on shooting at Aireborough. Must get my trusty physio, Rob Wilson, to have another look at it.

In the afternoon, I mark out a pitch for tomorrow's games against Weston Lane and try a gentle jog around the football pitch at the club. This doesn't seem to aggravate the pain at all, so the only problem now is kicking a ball.

Sunday 14th May.
Home to Weston Lane.

I've often wished, watching the boys play, that I could be nine years old again just for one match. To shrink myself down to the same size as Jimmy, Jack and the rest. I'd play in defence with Max and we'd be impassable. Or midfield with Jack and Josh, passing round the opposition like they weren't there. One-twos, keeping possession like Brazil. I'd cover the ferocious-tacking Matthew W in defence, allowing him to make forays forward. I'd slide inviting balls through for the forwards - Michael to show off his thunderbolt shooting and for Matthew M, watching him beat defenders for fun. I'd play with a relaxed confidence, knowing if we did get careless, Jimmy would save everything. I'd even score the winner myself - a right foot drive, scorching the net, after a move where the whole team had touched the ball at least once. It would be like the goal Carlos Alberto scored for Brazil in the 1970 World Cup Final. And just like Brazil, we'd be unbeatable, the talk of the town.

Today, the boys don't need me, or anyone else for that matter. They play as well as they've played all season. We're playing a side I like to use as our yardstick and at last we're competing on their level. Weston Lane are a very good side, but this morning we come out on top. It gives me a lot of pleasure to end the season in such style. Josh, who's captain for the day in probably his last game for us, scores the first goal against his old club. Typically, Matthew M gets two goals in his own impudent manner and Michael scores from close range, after an intelligent pass from Murray. It's a competitive match, with Weston Lane having almost as much possession as us. They're unlucky when a shot hits the bar and when another strikes a post, but finally score before the end to give a fairer reflection on the game overall.

Afterwards, it's nice to be complimented on my team's passing ability by their manager, Peter Atkinson. I thank him, whilst admitting my B team probably won't match theirs. As it turns out, I'm right. We lose 5-0, which proves that despite all our efforts from lads like Adam and James on the day and our overall progress this season, we still have a way to go before we can match the

78

great strength in depth of clubs like Weston Lane.

Monday 15th May.

I have a headache a bullet wouldn't cure. Must be the oppressive weather, which has got to blow a storm soon. The ground needs rain, as it's hard and bumpy, whilst the grass is long enough to trip me up and lose markers in.

It's the last training session of the season. Sixteen boys present and all pretty lively. We warm up first as usual and follow that with passing, volleys and headers in twos. We then practise a passing drill which incorporates making space and an angle for a pass. Despite a slight element of mischief in the air, it is still a worthwhile exercise.

After the small-sided game, we finish off the session with a penalty shoot-out. This is for fun and in case we've got to take them in the tournament on Sunday.

Tuesday 16th May.

A nightmare day when nothing goes right. I spend most of it driving around from one meeting to another, but people I'm supposed to see are either late or don't show up at all. Then to top it all, my car breaks down on the way to Burley to buy a bicycle for Joe. All of a sudden, there's a nasty smell from the engine, followed by great clouds of smoke. Two hours later and after much pacing about waiting for the breakdown services, the problem is temporarily patched up and I arrive an hour late for the meeting at the club. It's to organise stuff for the tournament at the weekend, but by the time I sit down, it's all but sorted. I take a look at the draw for the Under 9s competition and the A team, in particular, have got a tough group. Shame Josh can't play, I was beginning to feel quietly confident about our chances of winning. Now, I'm not so sure. Still, we're far from being a one man team and we are playing well at the moment. Of course we've a chance. But at times like these, I have to keep my own competitive nature in check and remind myself that winning isn't as important as the boys enjoying themselves.

Saturday 20th May.
It's the start of the Otley Tournament today. Under 8's, Under 10s and Under 12s. (Though due to a misunderstanding between Malcolm Dobinson and Richard Danskin, one of the Otley Under 12s teams is having to play in the tournament at Burley instead.)

I get down to the club by 7.00am to help put up nets and staple programmes together. Most of the hard work has already been done. The marking of thirteen pitches was done yesterday afternoon and evening. Although I wasn't able to spare the time to lend a hand, this doesn't stop one or two having a friendly dig at my late arrival.

At 9.00am, I grab a dodgy looking burger from the barbeque and leave the club in my dad's car to watch my son Joe compete at Burley. Several emotionally fraught hours later - which includes two lots of extra time and subsequent penalty shoot outs - I'm feeling proud as I watch Joe collect his runners-up medal from the Under 12s final.

On the way home, we catch the last twenty minutes of a rather flat looking F.A. Cup Final, before picking up my car from an almost deserted club at Otley Town. It seems the tournament went well and lots of money was made. Roll on tomorrow.

Sunday 21st May. The Otley Town Juniors 6-a-side Tournament.
At 6.00am, I'm awake with butterflies in my stomach. The last day of the season and I really, really want the boys to do well. It's the turn of the Under 9s, Under 11s and Under 13s and again, I'm down the club early, before 7.30am. There's not as much to do this morning, as everything, including goals and nets were left up overnight. Just a little clearing up from yesterday's mess before the cars start arriving. By 9.30am, the place is jammed with bodies. Managers are registering their teams, boys are

charging about in their different coloured strips awaiting the big kick-off and one or two unsuspecting spectators are sampling the delights from the barbeque. I spend my time moving my bag, balls and water bottles about, nervously waiting for my boys to turn up.

By 10.15am, the A team are kicking off the first of their Group One matches, against Whinmore A and the rollercoaster ride begins. Five minutes each way isn't a long time, when to do well your team must win most of the games to qualify for the quarter-finals. Barely thirty seconds from time, Michael produces a rocket of a shot and we win 1-0. From there, I rush over to the pitch opposite, where the B team draw their opening Group Four fixture 0-0 against Wigton Moor A.

Back and forward for the next three hours - from A team to B team, sorting them out, rotating players giving them all a fair chance of action and hardly having time to draw breath in the drizzling rain, never mind a cup of tea. The A team beat Weston Lane B 2-1, Eccleshill B 1-0, Clayton Clarets B 6-0, before drawing 2-2 with Long Lee A. We're in the next round, as runners-up to Long Lee, who've the same points as us, but a better goal difference. The B team draw 0-0 with Eccleshill A, win 1-0 against Wilsden B, draw 0-0 with Long Lee C and beat Clayton Clarets A 1-0. Amazingly, they have also qualified for the quarter-finals, as runners-up in their group. I am already more than happy with their achievement, but could the A team go all the way? The euphoria of it all is almost overwhelming. The parents, I can tell are enjoying it and Shane Waring, Matthew's dad, is already talking about finals and medals.

At 2.00pm, the B team take the field against Long Lee A. The first half lasts a lifetime, mainly because the referee forgets to check his watch. It's 0-0 at half-time, but after that my lads just can't hold out, despite a spirited attempt and lose 2-0. I feel disappointed for them, but proud at the same time. They've definitely achieved more than I expected.

The A team beat Shelf 2-0 and make it to the semi-finals. Now, all that remains between my Under 9s and a first final appearance, are the team those most 'in-the-know' are saying will win it: Eccleshill A. I try telling the boys to rest, but that's not easy when they're excited.

The other quarter-finals have now been played, so Jack comes up to me and asks, "Who won the game between Silsden and Silsden?"

81

Me: "Silsden."
Jack: "Oh."

Before the semi-final, I give them all one last team talk. They already know I think they've done great getting this far and whatever happens they should be pleased with themselves.

And so, with a healthy crowd cheering us on, we kick off. Within a couple of minutes, we're behind to a screamer of a goal that Jimmy barely sees. When another fierce shot hits our net before half-time, I know it's all over. I try to gee the boys up, but their body language has changed. From fiercely competitive and confident, the spark and belief has gone. By the end it's 3-0 and we're out. I heave a big sigh and gather the boys together in the middle of the pitch. There are some sad faces, but I tell them how proud I am and that we couldn't have played any better. Eccleshill certainly deserved to win and I expect they'll do well in the final. Their manager, Brian Cosherill comes over to us and says, "Never mind lads, but you were beaten by a good side."

I want to punch him, even though I'm sure he didn't mean to sound arrogant. I respond with, "You just beat a good side mate."

And when everyone else had slipped away, I noticed a quiet little lad stood beside me. "What's the matter Jimmy?" I said. " Are you OK?" But he just started crying, finally giving in to the disappoinment. So I gave him a hug and felt my eyes momentarily fill up as well. "Never mind. I'm disappointed too. But we got to the quarter-finals last year, the semi-finals this year. Next year we'll win it." And with that we went to get some sweets to cheer him up.

82

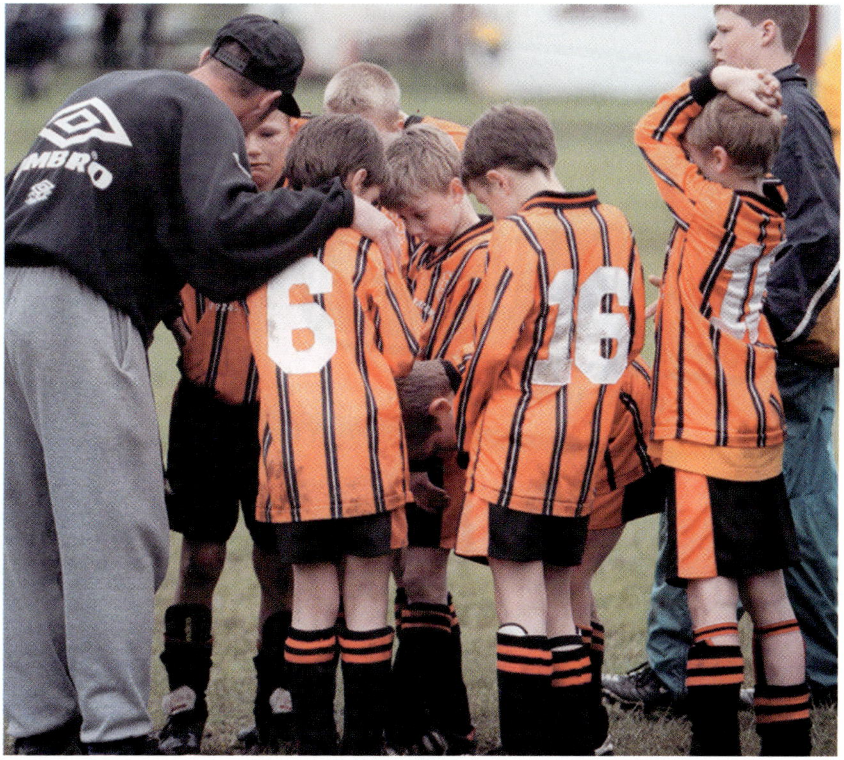
MBRO
6
16

OTLEY TOWN JUNIORS

OTLEY TOWN JUNIORS U'9s

Otley Town Juniors Under 9's are part of Otley Town Football Club and play their home games at the Old Showground, on Pool Road in Otley. This age group has two teams and was formed in 1997. They have been playing matches in the Norman Bairstow Friendly League for the past two seasons.

*****

JUNE

Friday 9th June.

Max is on a ten week invitation course at Leeds United, which I'm sure he'll do well on. Shane Waring is keen to get his son Matthew a chance too. All this, combined with Josh's involvement with Barnsley gives me a lot of mixed feelings to be honest. Firstly, I'm pleased for the boys, who must be excited and should make the most of their opportunity. In the case of Max, I take special pride, as I've coached him for three years. On the other hand, I could be losing a few great kids who, because of their commitments to these clubs, won't be able to play with their mates. And they will be hard to replace. Don't get me wrong, I think it's a great policy for the professional clubs like Leeds to try and develop talent early - so long as they look after the boys they eventually don't want. But what do the feeder clubs like ours get out of it? I heard recently that local side Menston had lost boys to Leeds United. The same has happened to Wyke with Man. United and I'm sure other clubs have similar experiences. Personally, I feel all of these big clubs have a big responsibility and a moral obligation to give something back to little outfits like ours. Doesn't have to be money, even though it would be great to help develop the sporting facilities in Otley, which are nothing short of scandalous. It could be equipment or some free coaching time. If that sort of relationship became the norm, I would feel a lot more sympathetic to these situations than I do now.

Sunday 11th June.

I have taken it upon myself to generate interest in an Under 7s and Under 8s football section at Otley for next season. I feel it is important to establish football from an early age within the club and have therefore organised a free coaching session. Although I don't plan to extend myself to running more than next year's Under 10s, I hope that after seeing the set-up at Otley and the number of boys showing interest, a couple of would-be managers will come forward to run the sides. A guy called Dave Walker, who's son is here, reckons he's interested.

Martin Ibbetson, Otley Town's first team manager, helps me with the coaching, which is just as well. Eighteen lads turn up - more than I expected. Looking at his face afterwards, I think he's glad he doesn't have to work with boys this young every week! Nevertheless, it all goes pretty well and with a potential manager on the scene, I think we're in business.

Wednesday 14th June.

I pop in to see John Hutchinson, who's done a great job in producing all the photographic material for this book. He's a football fan too and with the European Championships in full swing, we inevitably get to talking about England's chances against Germany on Saturday. I think it's one game we might just win, although John's worried. "Why?" I ask him. "The Germans aren't that good at the moment." To which John replies, "Yeah, but we never win on ITV."

Saturday 17th June.

Just out of mischievous curiosity, I watch the match on ITV instead of BBC1 and unbelievably England win 1-0. Just goes to show what John knows about football.

Tuesday 20th June.

England go out of Euro 2000. They're two minutes from a place in the quarter-finals, when they gift Romania a penalty - from which they score to win. Football can be cruel sometimes, though England can have no complaints really. Romania, like so many of the teams in the tournament, were a good footballing side. They passed the ball better than England. Kept the ball better than England. Were more inventive than England. Sad to say.

Friday 23rd June. The Otley Town Juniors Presentation Night.

I've prepared my speech, my manager's report for the season and I've had a pint of Guinness to calm the nerves. We're at the Otley Social Club and about two hundred or so people are present.

When it's my turn up on stage, I paint a glowing report on the performances of my Under 9 boys and then present each lad with a trophy for taking part. Max Milner wins the Players' Player of the Year Award for the second year in succession, Matthew McGlinchey gets my Player of the Year for the A team, whilst Adam Walker gets it for the B team. I could have given the Manager's Award to any one of several boys. Max or Jack. Josh or Matthew Waring if they'd played more matches. It was a tough one and in a way, I'd like to have given the lot of them an extra something, because each and every one has improved no end.

I think I've learned a lot too, which is important. Like the players though, I want to get better, so I'll have to sit down in the summer and work out some new challenges for myself.

For now, I can relax and reflect on a memorable season that's also been thoroughly enjoyable.

✺✺✺✺✺✺

Since 1961, it has been part of Everton folklore that when the team is struggling, the Goodison crowd will shout out to the beleaguered manager, "Fetch a taxi!" It was in that year the then Everton chairman John Moores, sensationally dismissed manager John Carey in the back of a taxi cab.

As I step off stage tonight, Chris Baker presents me with an envelope on behalf of all the players and parents. Inside is a card and another smaller envelope. When I spot the words "Taxi fare," written big in biro on the front, I fear the worst. Maybe despite our successful season, it was felt not good enough. The A team had only finished third in the league. The B team eighth in their division. Maybe they had expected more. Maybe they'd had a meeting and decided enough was enough. Maybe they were now taking action and had someone else lined up as my replacement.

In the modern, cutthroat, win-or-suffer-the-consequences world of professional football, it would have been the sack. Inside my envelope was a message of thanks with a credit for a meal at a local Italian restaurant. And the money for a taxi ride home.

✺✺✺✺✺✺

Otley U-9s A........6
Idle Saints............0
A convincing win but even more pleasing a fine team performance came from Town Under-9s A. Though Idle tried hard Otley's superior work rate and passing was the key to this victory. Matthew McGlinchey scored the opening goal after beating two defenders and he then added a second. Sean Brotherton went close with a shot on the turn and was unlucky again a few moments later.
Matthew Waring, who had an outstanding game, then scored a third after good approach play by Jack Wood.
Max Milner added a fourth before half-time. In the second period a great run and shot by Michael Beecroft was only parried by the 'keeper and Jack Wood struck the ball home. Several dangerous corner kicks almost provided further goals before James Dalby slotted home the sixth.
Otley U-9s B.......7
Cullingworth......5
This was a most amazing game which the home side started brightly with an early goal from Murray Simm. Cullingworth then took control scoring four times, two either side of half-time.
At 4-1 down the match looked over for the home side but debutant Josh Waite had other ideas. Coolly slotting home from close range he drove home a second from distance before scoring a third to level at 4-4.
Waite was now looking menacing with every touch and he linked up well with Simm. Another strong run forward gave Waite his fourth and Otley the lead.
Cullingworth then hit back and mistake in the Town defence saw them equalise. Back came Otley with Adam Walker and Callum Shaw providing the ammunition for Waite to score his fifth goal and restore Otley's advantage.
Good work by Louis Christoforan gave Lloyd Almond the chance to seal a remarkable 7-5 win.
Otley U-9s C............0
Cullingworth B......2
Town Juniors entertain Hessle
Otley U-9s A............7
Hessle A...............0
Otley U-9s B..............7
Hessle B...............1
IDLE SAINTS U-9S..........0 OTLEY U-9S A..........4
OTLEY U-9S A
COWLING U-9S
SHIPLEY A..........1 OTLEY TOWN U-9S A
OTLEY U-9S 'A'..........3 SHIPLEY 'A'